ROMEO AND JULIET ARE SANDRO BOTTICELLI AND SIMONETTA VESPUCCI

By Stephane Baillon

"Romeo and Juliet" by William Shakespeare, published in 1597 was taken from the book "Giulietta e Romeo" by Da Porto dating from 1530, itself taken from the book "Mariotto e Ganozza" by Masuccio Salernitano written in 1478.

These two characters, Romeo and Juliet, loving each other deeply when it was forbidden to them, truly existed. Juliet was called in real life Simonetta Vespucci and Romeo was called Sandro Botticelli. Here is their story

STEPHANE BAILLON

Copyright 2022 Stephane Baillon

CHAPTER 1

1430 A.D

The story begins 15 years before Sandro was born.

At this time, Cosimo de Medici was at war with other families in the city of Florence.

Cosimo de Medici is imprisoned and even sentenced to death. But Cosimo de Medici is a very clever man and a remarkable political strategist. He skillfully managed to turn the situation to his advantage, and then recapture the city of Florence to govern it.

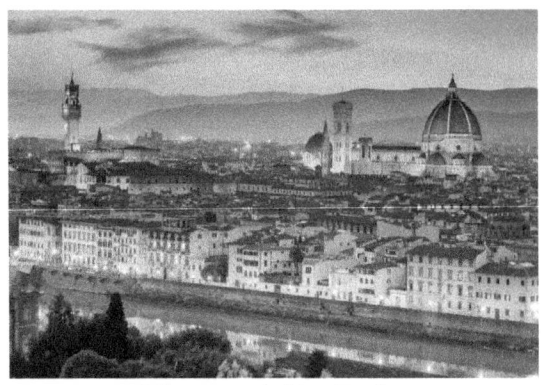

Florence city, Italy

Cosimo de Medici is a very cultured man who collects books of all ideological thoughts.

You have to put yourself in the historical context of that time. 1430 is the end of the Middle Ages and the Christian power is still very strong in Italy with the inquisition which burns in public place all those who think differently from the biblical texts. Nevertheless, several ideological currents circulate in Italy, in particular the texts of ancient Greek philosophers.

Cosimo de Medici is a person who makes a pact with the church and who even has an excellent relationship with the pope who allowed him to take over the city of Florence, but he is also an intellectual who wants to push the limits of thought and philosophy.

CHAPTER 2

1439 A.D

Cosimo de Medici welcomes in Florence city an exiled philosopher, condemned to death by the church, who is called Plethon.
This philosopher is nicknamed the second Plato as his ideas are so close to Plato.
Cosimo de Medici is amazed by Plethon's words and thoughts, so much so that Plethon becomes Cosimo de Medici's philosophical mentor.

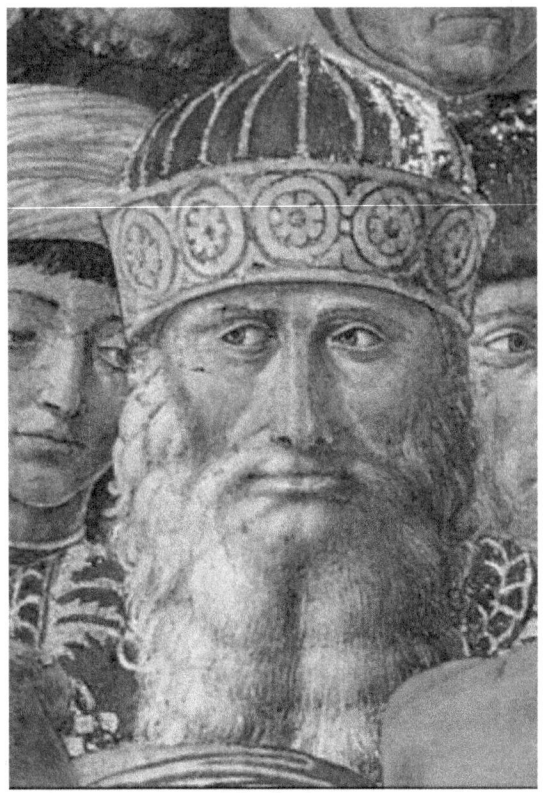

Plethon

Thus, the friends of Cosimo de Medici are humanists, intellectuals and thinkers such as Marsilio Ficino, Jean Pic de la Mirandole, Politien and Bienivieni but also artists and painters such as Fra Filippo Lippi.

CHAPTER 3

1445 A.D

Birth of Sandro Botticelli in the Ognissanti district of Florence. Her father is a tanner but they are not poor. He is the fourth son of a family of tanners and goldsmiths.

Unfortunately, he has health problems, he cannot do the same things as other boys and he has to stay at home. He spends his childhood reading. He is nicknamed by all his family "the one who reads".

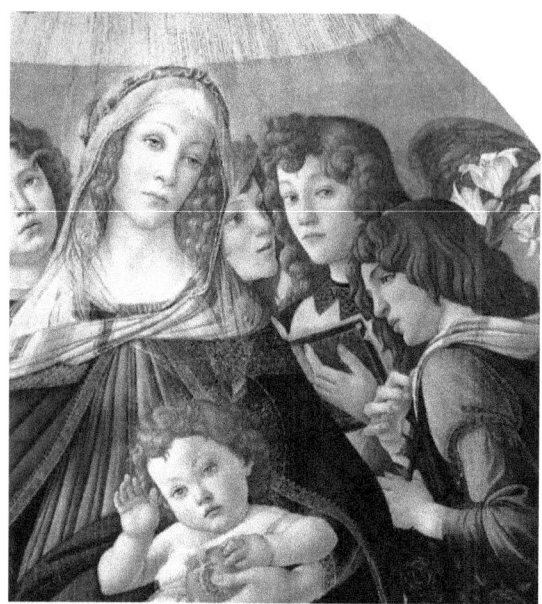

Sandro Botticelli painted by himself, looking at the viewer and holding a book in his hand.

CHAPTER 4

1459 A.D

Cosimo de Medici, in honor of his master of thought Plethon, creates "the neoplatonist academy of Florence" and he asks his friend Marsilio Ficino to translate all of Plato's texts into Italian. Gutenberg has just invented this revolutionary machine which allows the very easy reproduction of books, the printing press. Sandro Botticelli is 14 years old and he has already read everything so, these new texts by Plato which circulate in Florence city thanks to this new printing process are obviously devoured by Sandro Botticelli whose first passion is reading. The young Sandro Botticelli will approach this neoplatonist academy and his great intelligence is not long in being noticed. At that time, Cosimo de Medici was 70 years old and he met Sandro Botticelli, 14 years old.

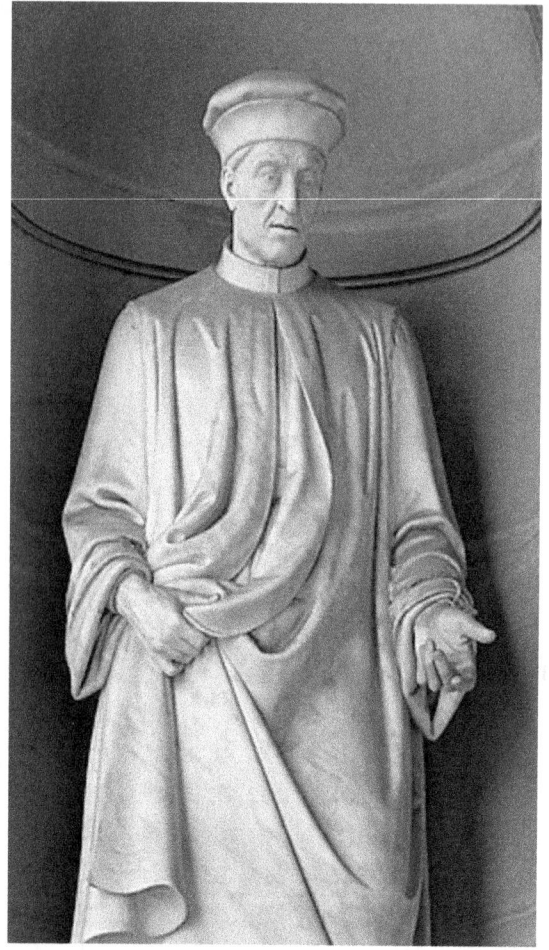

Cosimo di Medici

The intellect meeting the intellect, a special and very strong relationship is born between these two persons, Sandro Botticelli and Cosimo de Medici, inhabited by a kind of similar thought. Cosimo does something totally unusual by taking under his protection this young man who is not part of a powerful Florentine family. At the same time, the painter Fra Filippo Lippi had problems with ecclesiastical justice. He asked a sister to pose for him and he fell in love with her. From their forbidden union is born a child, a boy. Because of this forbidden relationship, Fra Filippo Lippi is condemned to death by the church but Cosimo saves his friend thanks to his privileged relations with the Pope. Cosimo asks his friend Fra Filippo Lippi to take the young Sandro Botticelli as his pupil and disciple to train him in painting. Sandro Botticelli is not part of the Medici family but, incredibly, he quickly becomes Cosimo's spiritual son. Sandro is introduced to Peter de Medici, the son of Cosimo and to Lorenzo de Medici, his 10-year-old grandson. Sandro quickly impressed all these major historical figures with his extraordinary intelligence, his culture, his numerous artistic talents and his genius. He gains self-confidence and Cosimo sees him as his ideological successor, as if he's handing over something to him. In a few years, from the age of 14 to 19, Sandro was introduced to all the thinkers, humanists and intellectuals of Florence who were close to Cosimo de Medici and Sandro immersed himself in Neoplatonism while painting with his painting master, Fra Filippo Lippi.

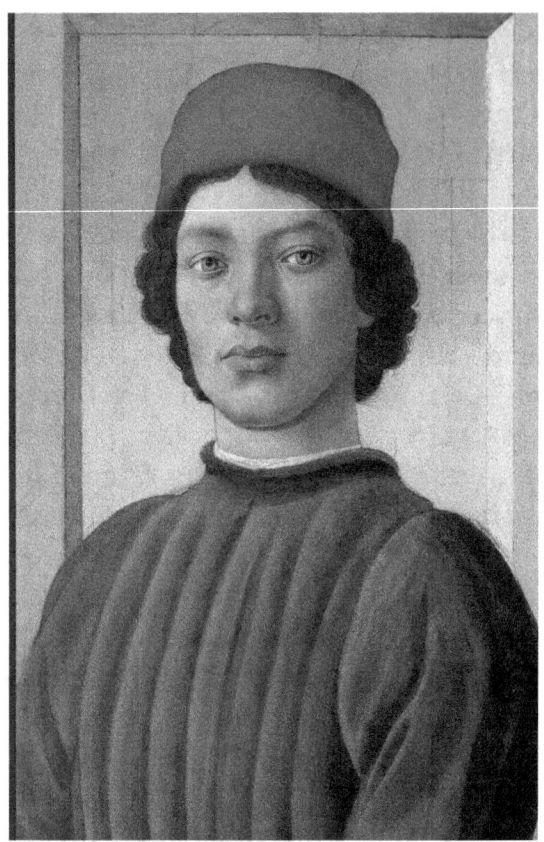

**Sandro Botticelli, 17 years old,
painted by Fra Filippo Lippi.**

At that time, apart from portraits, it was only allowed to paint religious artworks. Anyone who did not paint religious artworks was burned at the stake in the public square. Yet Cosimo de Medici had managed the feat of circulating Plato's thoughts in Florence city that were totally different from the Christian religion while being politically close to the very powerful Catholic dogma.

CHAPTER 5

1464 A.D

Cosimo de Medici is known in history for having, throughout his life, spent a lot of money in support of artists, poets and humanists. The word "patronage" is associated with his name even today. But, this year 1464, at the age of 74, Cosimo de Medici died.

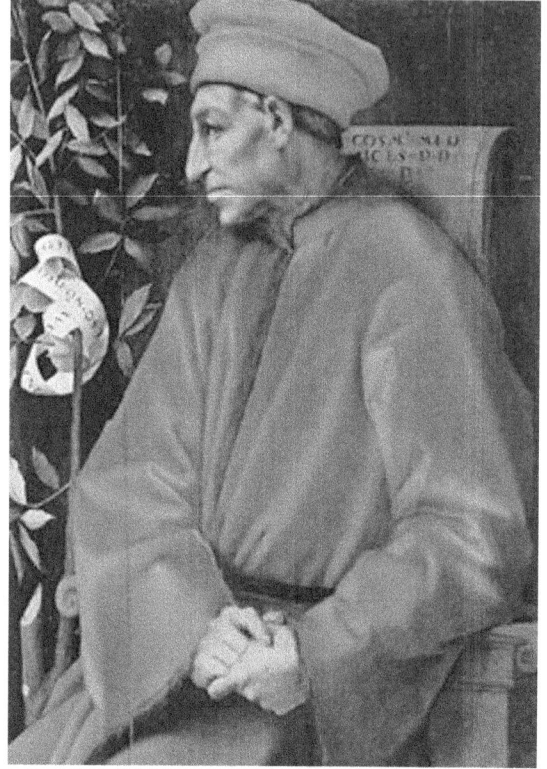

Cosimo di Medici

His son Peter, who has his father in admiration, takes up the torch and he wants to perpetuate the work of his father and continues the patronage of artists, poets and thinkers in Florence city. Thus, his son, Lorenzo de Medici grew up with this continuity and the presence of Sandro Botticelli that Peter de Medici greatly appreciated.

ROMEO AND JULIET ARE SANDRO BOTTICELLI AND SIMON...

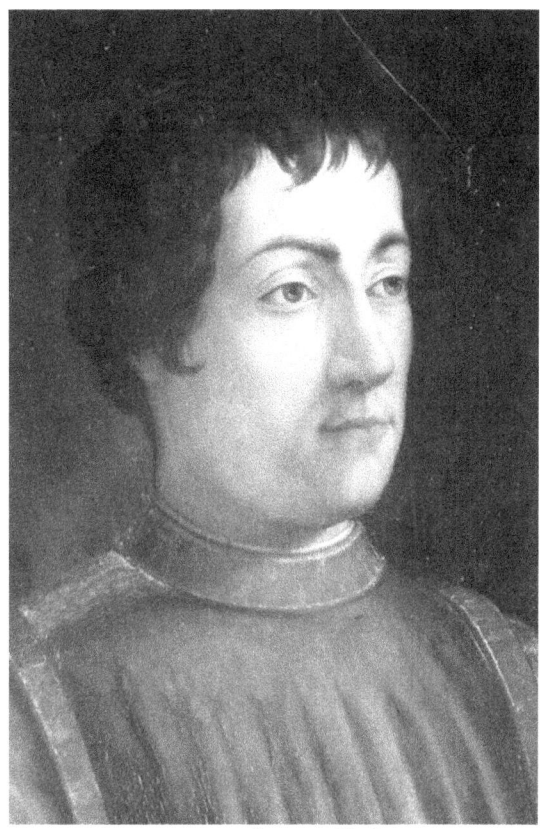

Peter de Medici

CHAPTER 6

1467 A.D

Sandro Botticelli is in Andrea del Verrocchio's studio. This workshop is called the "laboratory". There are a dozen artists who carry out all kinds of commissions. There are, of course, religious paintings but, also sculptures, statues of horses with soldiers on them, giant bells to produce and decorate, in short, there is everything in this workshop which has the goal to achieve the impossible. Among the artists present this year 1467 in the workshop of Verrocchio there is Sandro Botticelli, 22 years old.

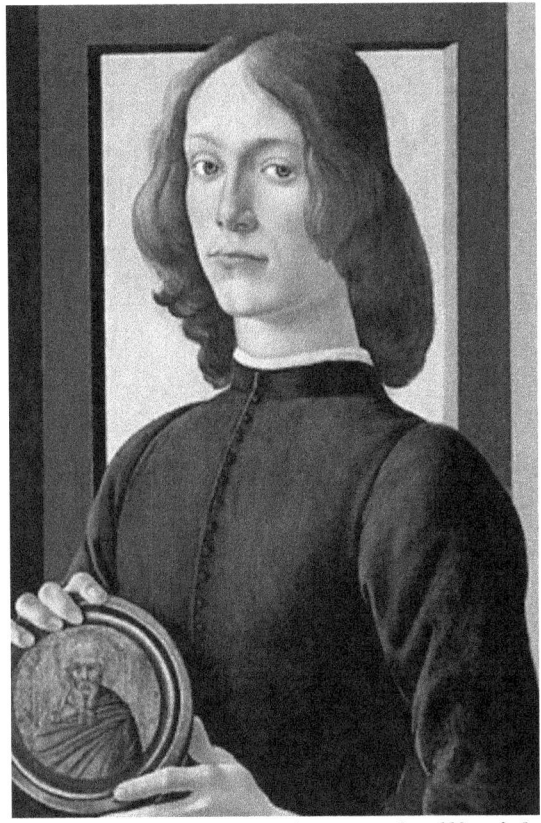

Self-portrait by Sandro Botticelli with a portrait of Plethon in his hands

But there is also in Andrea del Verrocchio's studio a young man of 17 called Perugino, who excels in painting and another young man of 15 who has just joined the studio who's name is Leonardo and who comes from the city "Vinci". Usually, Leonardo should not have joined Andrea del Verrocchio's studio at 15, but he insisted so much, even offering to clean other people's brushes for free that Verrocchio finally accepted. In this year 1467 we are therefore in the presence of the three greatest geniuses of painting in the same workshop at the same time. It is obvious that such geniuses immediately found affinities with each other. Sandro is the oldest and the most experienced but Perugino and Leonardo have this ability to learn very quickly and are already showing great talent but they are still very young. Sandro, 22, already has exceptional abilities from an artistic point of view since his master was the very talented Fra Filippo Lippi. Moreover, Sandro has a great knowledge with all his readings and he has the very strong support of the Medici family. Perugino and Leonardo see in Sandro an amazing artist, a genius, a model of success and they are lucky enough to be able to share the creations of amazing artworks with him in Andrea del Verrocchio's studio. For Sandro Botticelli, everything is important in artwork, even the smallest details reveal capital importance. Sandro applies himself to the hands, which are very important to him, but also to the details of the writings in the books and even the attitudes of the characters he draws. He explains to his friends how to bring out a character by the gaze directed towards the spectator or directed towards a place or another person. Perugino and Leonardo also imbibe the importance of these details. I think that a strong friendship was, this year 1467, between these three artists whom the world today calls geniuses. Here is a painting by Sandro Botticelli

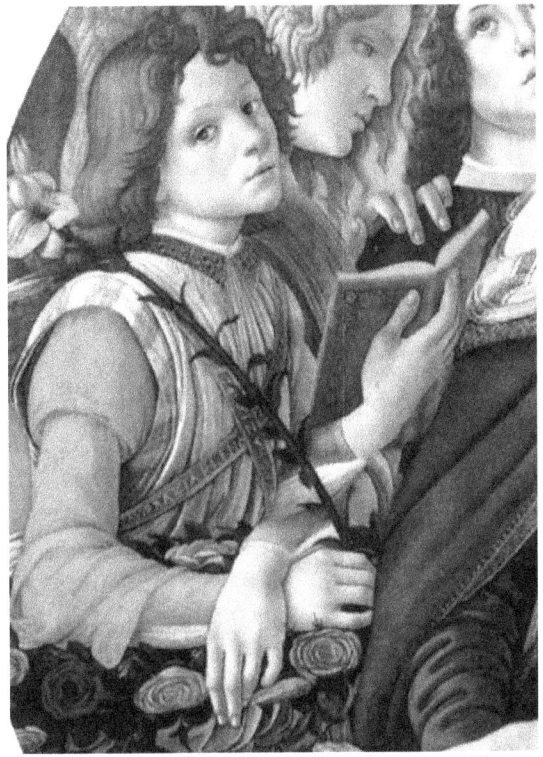

Painting from Sandro Botticelli

See how the details are marked with regards to the intricacy of the hands, fingers and the entanglement of one hand over another with a slight flexion of the wrist. This technique of Sandro will be taken up by Perugino.

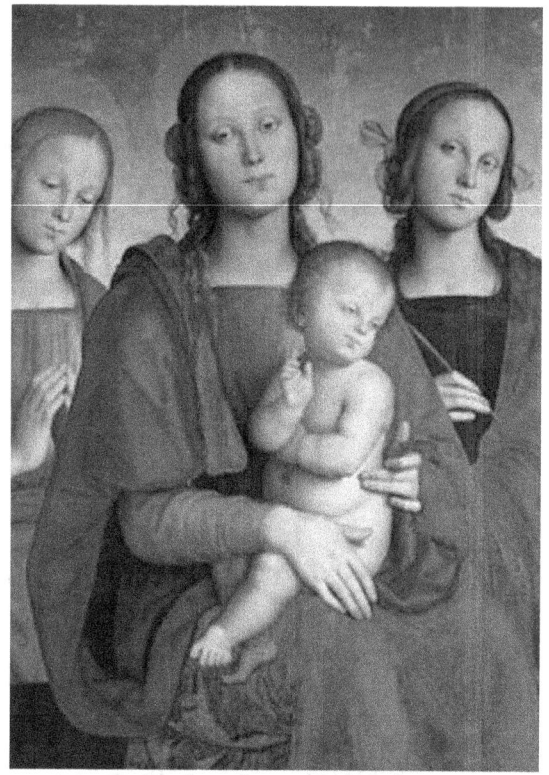

Painting from Perugino

But also by Leonardo .

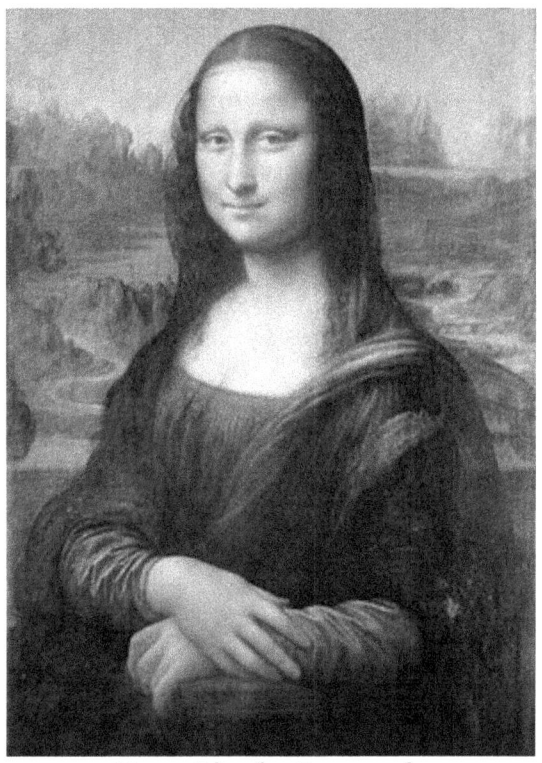

Mona Lisa by Leonardo

Note the almost perfect similarity in these paintings by these three artists. It is obvious that Sandro Botticelli shared his techniques with Perugino and Leonardo. Thus, for two years, all these artists lived together in Andrea del Verrocchio's studio and refined their artistic talents by sharing their painting techniques.

CHAPTER 7

1469 A.D

A grand wedding is brewing. One of the powerful and ancient Florentine families, the Vespucci, is finishing preparations for the wedding of the year. One of the Vespucci sons, Marco, met a girl in Genoa, on a university trip, and he is going to get married. The future bride is said to be amazingly beautiful, her name is Simonetta and she is very young, she is 16 years old. The Vespucci have been very close to the Medici for a long time and these families are allies. The Medici were the richest and most powerful and organized, for their friends, the Vespucci family, the most grandiose wedding ceremony in the most beautiful palaces of Florence city. All the greatest Italian families are invited to this grandiose wedding where the Medici demonstrate their power and their fortune. Cosimo de Medici unfortunately died but his son Peter continues his father's work and his son, Lorenzo de Medici, 20, is on the way to becoming a major figure in Florence city and he will marry Clarisse Orsini, another powerful italian family, 2 months later. Peace and happiness reign over Florence city. The guests are hand-picked because everyone wants to attend this exceptional event, this wedding so amazing, so dazzling that it will mark history. Sandro Botticelli, 24, is some kind of part of the Medici family and he is invited by Peter de Medici to this great wedding to which he certainly invites his friends Perugino, 19, and Leonardo, 17. At this wedding is also present Amerigo Vespucci, 16, the cousin of Marco Vespucci, and whose name will be given to the American continent. All these beautiful people are very well dressed and these people are all very educated with this humanist and neoplatonist current which circulates in Florence city. Sandro is very smart just like Perugino and Leonardo. But are also present at this wedding, the humanists, philosophers and Italian thinkers Marsilio Ficino, Jean Pic de la Mirandole, Politien and Bienivieni, those who knew Cosimo de Medici very well and who saw Sandro Botticelli grow up. Giorgio Antonio Vespucci is also a humanist who knows all the other humanists and introduces them to his nephew, Amerigo Vespucci. It is therefore in an environment of power and money but also very intellectual that Simonetta is about to discover by marrying the Vespucci family in Florence city.

Except from Marco Vespucci and his family, no one has ever seen the future bride but rumors circulate about her extraordinary beauty, her incredible charm, her amazing natural grace. There are many people in the crowded church waiting for the bride. The impatience is palpable. The bride makes her grand entrance in her immaculate dress. The restraint of education means that no sound comes to disturb the music of the musicians but everyone is stunned and impressed by the extraordinary beauty of this woman who walks towards the altar in her long white dress. On her way, the whole room filled with the greatest Italian families, but also European princes and kings bows. At least, everyone except one, Sandro Botticelli, who remains standing up, petrified, watching this very beautiful woman move forward. She notices him and their eyes meet. The bride nevertheless continues on her way to the altar where she joins her future husband, Marco Vespucci. We are in the middle of a major diplomatic incident. Everyone in the cathedral noticed that Sandro had remained standing, petrified at the sight of this woman's beauty. All the texts concerning this marriage mention this major diplomatic "incident". Nevertheless, Sandro, being protected by Peter de Medici, there were no consequences to "this effrontery" but everyone noticed it that day. The Vespuccis are from the Ognissanti district of Florence city and Sandro Botticelli also lives in the Ognissanti district, he was born there, there is his whole family. Sandro Botticelli and Simonetta Vespucci would cross paths in the near future.

CHAPTER 8

1470 A.D

Only one year after the big wedding, Sandro decides to have his own workshop. Such a practice was not usual. 25 was considered too young to become a master painter but he did it anyway. His first commission entitled "the strength" gave off something strong and immediately he had phenomenal success with this first commission.

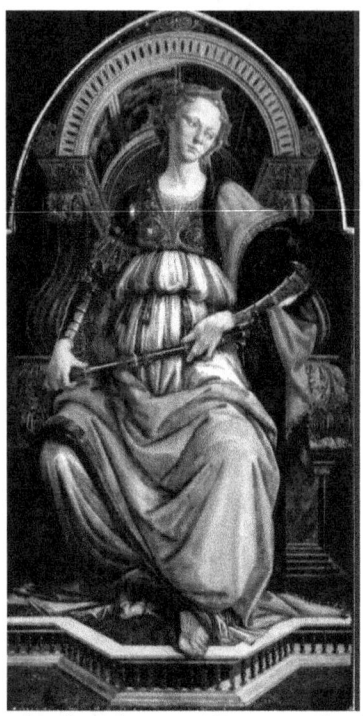

First painting by Sandro Botticelli as a master entitled "The Strenght"

He has the support of the Medici family, of all the humanists and all powerful families in Florence city, so the orders flow in. For all the other artists, Sandro is considered as a star, a complete artist who has fame and fortune. Sandro Botticelli is known for his allegories, that is to say that he likes to hide Greek mythologies, humanist and neoplatonist clues in religious artworks when it is strictly forbidden by Church. Moreover, he is criticized for modifying paintings ordered to his own style but he is so gifted, so talented, that it even becomes a signature.

Sandro put messages in this painting and also people by including the major characters of this period. This is "the adoration of the Magi"

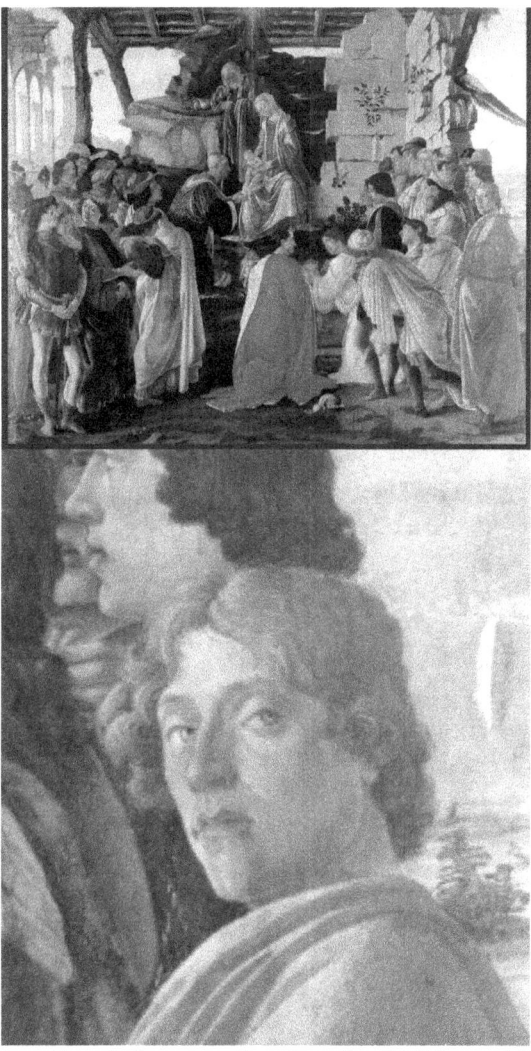

On the right, Sandro Botticelli himself.

STEPHANE BAILLON

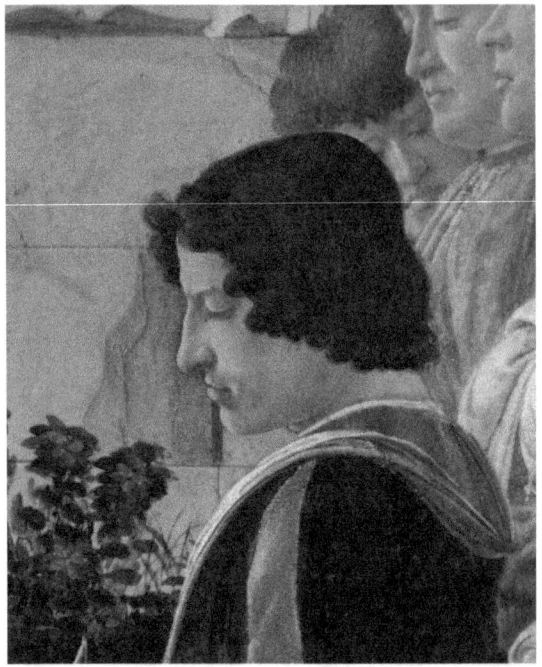

In front of him, Lorenzo de Medici

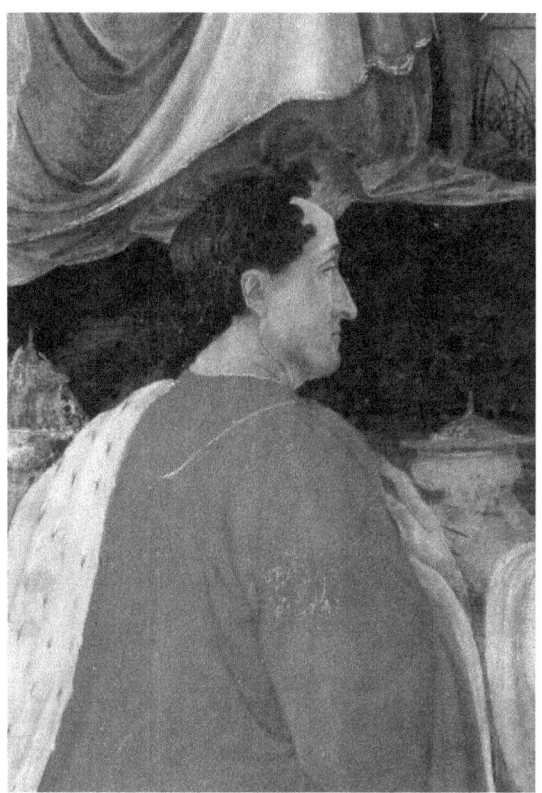

In the center, kneeling and dressed in red, Peter de Medici.

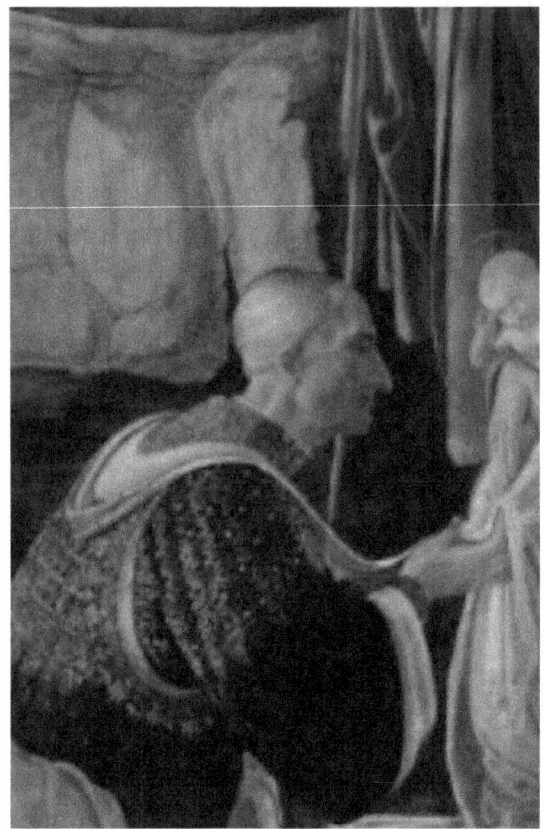

The one on his knees, with gray hair, closest to the child and to Mary, is Cosimo de Medici.

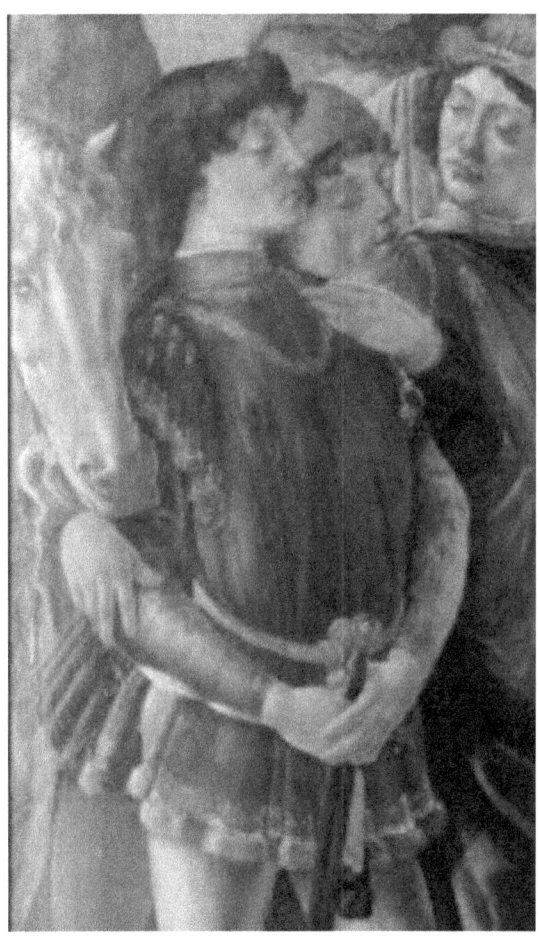

On the left of the painting, with his haughty air,
Julian de Medici, his friends, his horse, his sword.

CHAPTER 9

1474 A.D

Sandro Botticelli is 29 years old and he has been very successful for 4 years. He is a star in Florence city. Commissions flowed in and his artistic talent was recognized by all. He is the new master of painting in Florence city and he is totally independent because he has his master painting studio.

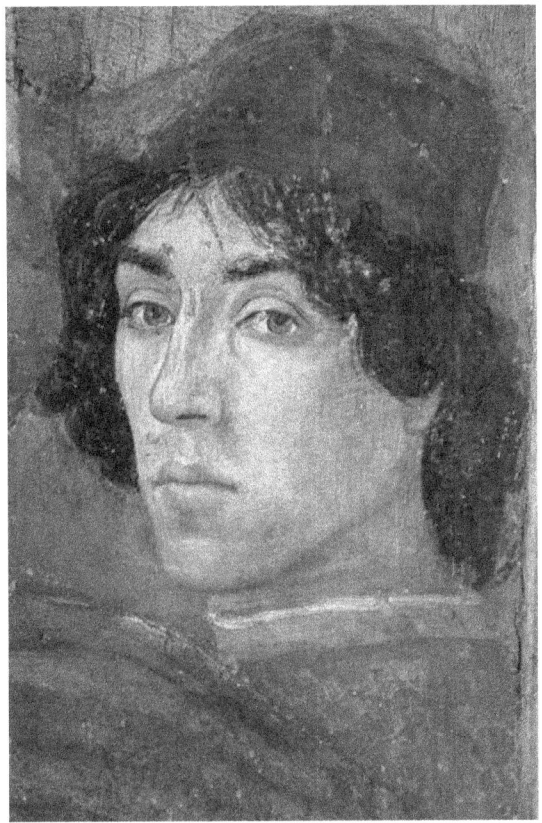

Portrait of Sandro Botticelli by Filippino Lippi

Simonetta Vespucci is 21 years old and she has been married to Marco Vespucci for 5 years. Her grace and intelligence are also very noticeable. Her popularity and beauty are at their peak. She is considered as the most beautiful woman in Italy and Europe.

STEPHANE BAILLON

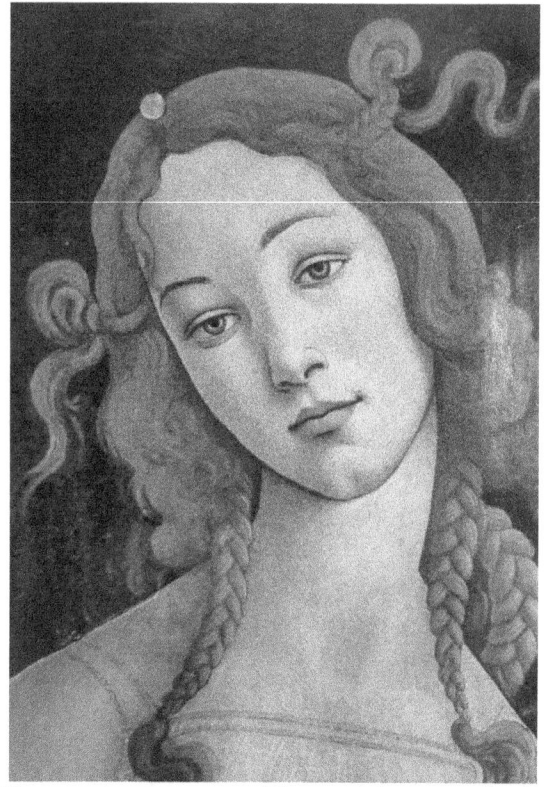

Simonetta Vespucci by Sandro Botticelli

CHAPTER 10

After the untimely death of Peter de Medici, his eldest son, Lorenzo de Medici, 25, is the new head of the Medici family and he has taken over the business of the Medici family with flying colors. He is a very clever man and a fine strategist like his grandfather Cosimo de Medici. He is young but already a skilled politician.

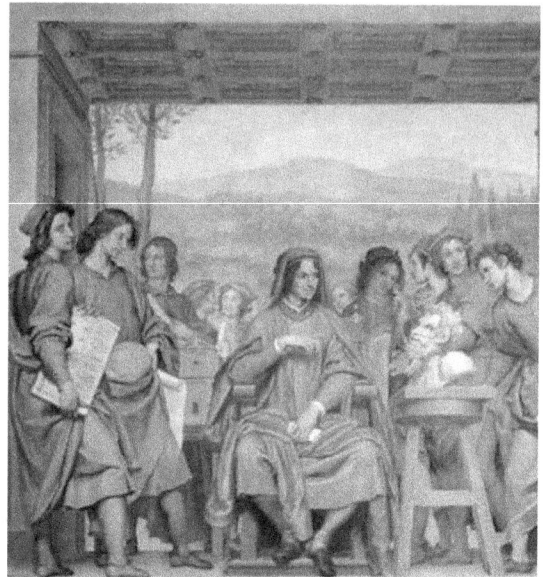

Lorenzo de' Medici seated in the center by Ottavio Vannini. Sandro on the left, red hat.

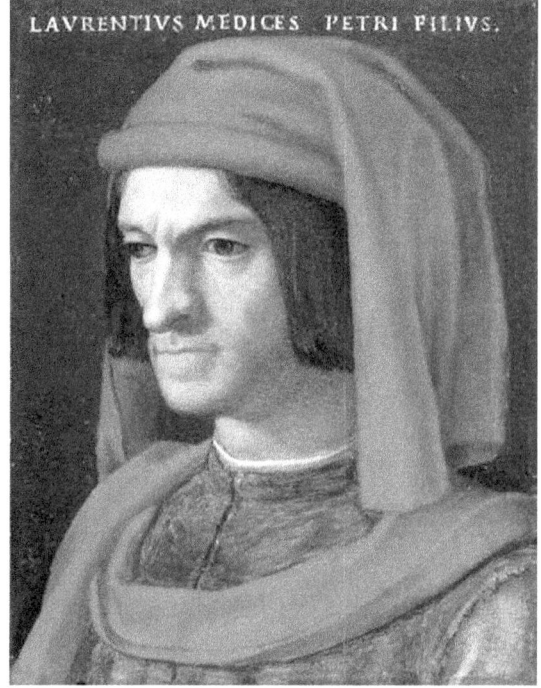

Lorenzo de Medici

Lorenzo likes the company of the sublime Simonetta Vespucci, this amazing woman, and he is very admiring, in love of course, like all the men, nobles and princes of this time who are close to the most beautiful woman in the world.

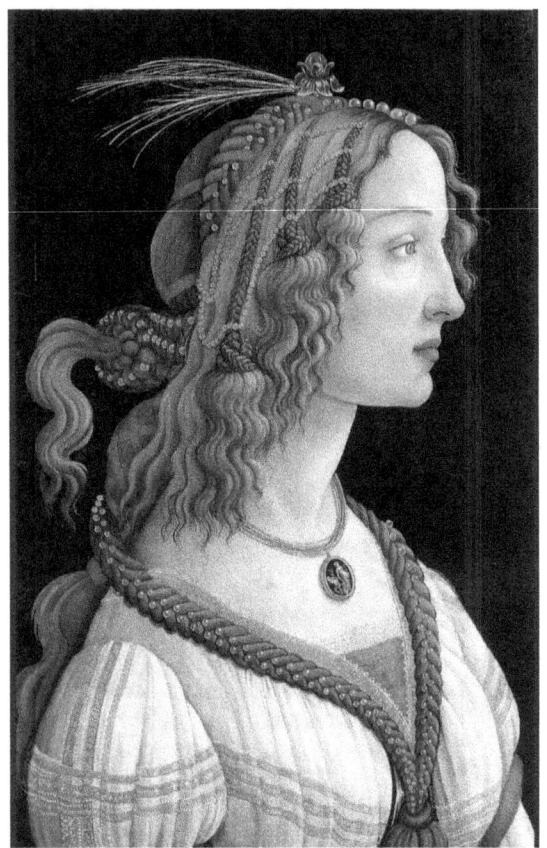

Simonetta Vespucci by Sandro Botticelli

But, Lorenzo de Medici is married to Clarisse Orsini and does not cross the limit. Lorenzo de Medici is a clever and respectful man for whom the name and the honor of the Medici family prevails above all else, so, there is no attempt by Lorenzo de Medici to cross moral limits and he does everything to preserve the strong alliance between the Medici, the Vespucci and the Orsini, guaranteeing peace and prosperity in Florence city.

CHAPTER 11

Closer

For 4 years, Sandro and Simonetta have been living in the same city, Florence, inhabiting the same district of Ognissanti and frequenting the same influential people in Florence city, the humanists and the Medici family. For 4 years, Sandro and Simonetta have been invited to the same banquets, attend the same festivities organized by the Medici. The Vespuccis are an allied family of the Medicis and Sandro has been the star artist protege of the Medicis for 15 years, he is a bit like a big brother for Lorenzo de Medici. Sandro is 29 years old, Lorenzo, 25 years old. They have known each other since childhood. At that time Sandro Botticelli was the superstar of painting but also of philosophical thought. For 15 years, he was very close to the greatest thinkers and philosophers of Florence city. Sandro not only has an exceptional artistic talent but a spirit, an extraordinary intellect, pushing the limits of thought. Cosimo de Medici had detected something so special in Sandro that he made Sandro his spiritual son by opening all doors to him.

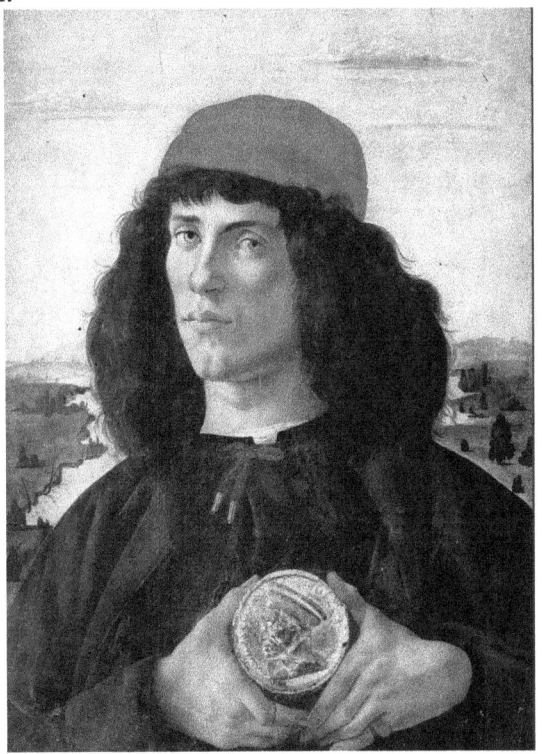

Self-portrait by Sandro Botticelli in homage to Cosimo de' Medici.

Florence is an exception at this time in Italy and Europe, under the control of the Pope and the Christian Church but with ideas of Neoplatonist Greek philosophies from the texts of the great Greek philosophers and mathematicians brought by

Cosimo de Medici. Sandro uses allegory a lot in his paintings, he puts a lot of hidden messages, coded messages. A look, a finger pointing to a clue, an open book, a text written in Greek, a title of a painting, Sandro was at that time the master of allegory in paintings and he was to strongly inspire Perugino, 26 and Leonardo Da Vinci, 22 years on this path of hiding clues in paintings. Sandro also uses mathematics in his paintings, inspired by ancient Greek mathematicians and modern Italian mathematicians who were very advanced in the field of mathematics. Sandro finds that the use of mathematics gives additional strength to artworks. Perugino and Leonardo also study mathematics as does their friend, their role model, Sandro Botticelli. Leonardo is interested in a certain "Vitruvius" who had mapped all the gigantic structures of antiquity, such as the Greek temples or the pyramids of Egypt. Sandro does not stop there, he studies Greek myths and mythologies but also the legends of antiquity and likes to tell stories of major characters, in particular female characters who have marked history. Sandro, whose genius overflows everywhere, is in love with Simonetta Vespucci, like all men of that time.

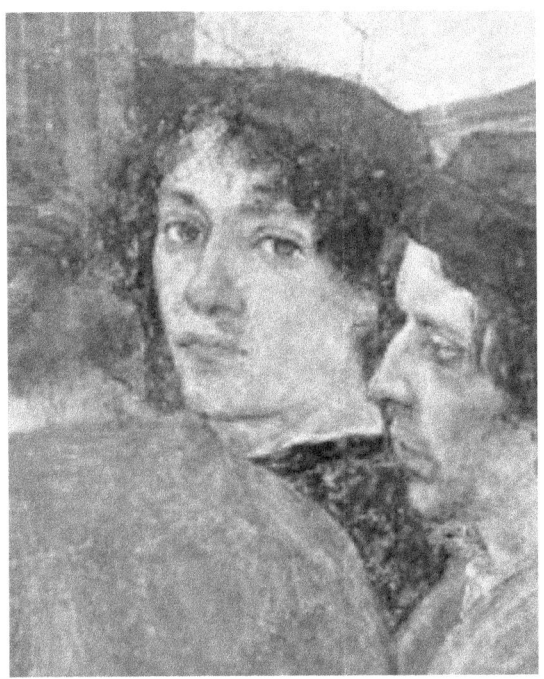

Sandro Botticelli by Filippino Lippi.

But a relationship between Simonetta Vespucci and Sandro Botticelli is totally forbidden at this time in Italy. She comes from a noble family and he is a simple painter, a forbidden union, absolutely unthinkable. It's all about family, prestige and honor at this time in Italy. There are those who belong to the great families, the nobility, who are everything and the others who are nothing. The honor of great families would never have supported a woman of the highest Italian nobility, who is moreover the most beautiful woman in Italy, the jewel of Florence city, to be in a relationship with a simple painter of the people. But, Sandro is not afraid of anything or anyone, he is a very handsome man, very elegant, very talented, very cultured and amazingly clever.

CHAPTER 12

By dint of being closer, even in a formal way, Sandro seduces Simonetta Vespucci. For him, only this woman exists, only she makes his heart beat so hard. He shows himself to be pleasant and attentive towards her, while being restrained due to her rank and her celebrity. Simonetta Vespucci has been married for 5 years to Marco Vespucci but the latter has extramarital relationships with other women. Simonetta lives in a gilded prison where divorce is not allowed, honor being predominant in Italy. Before the grace and incredible beauty of Simonetta Vespucci, all men are obviously in awe of this woman. The various European princes, the kings of the time, all admired this woman of incredible beauty and amazing natural grace.

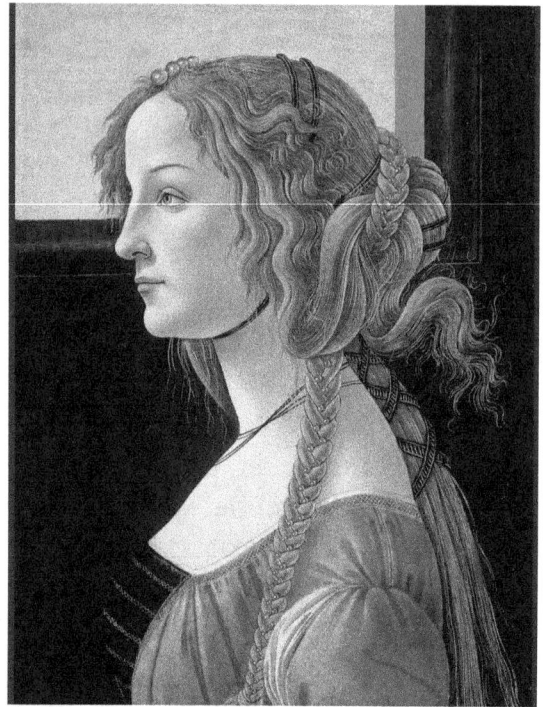

Simonetta Vespucci by Sandro Botticelli

However, inexorably, she begins to get closer to this brilliant, amazing artist, Sandro Botticelli. But, Sandro does not come from a noble Italian family so he is nothing, but he is so great that he surpasses all other princes and kings in Simonetta's eyes. It must be said that Sandro is really someone exceptional, already, at 14 years old, Cosimo de Medici had detected in him a unique potential and he had almost adopted Sandro.

Sandro respects women and admires them. Joan of Arc left indelible traces in Europe and Sandro is a big fan of her. He drew her in armor in his first painting entitled "the strength". Sandro is familiar with ancient myths such as that of Judith of Bethulia, this woman who saved an entire city through intelligence, cunning but also strength by beheading General Holofernes, saving thousands of villagers.

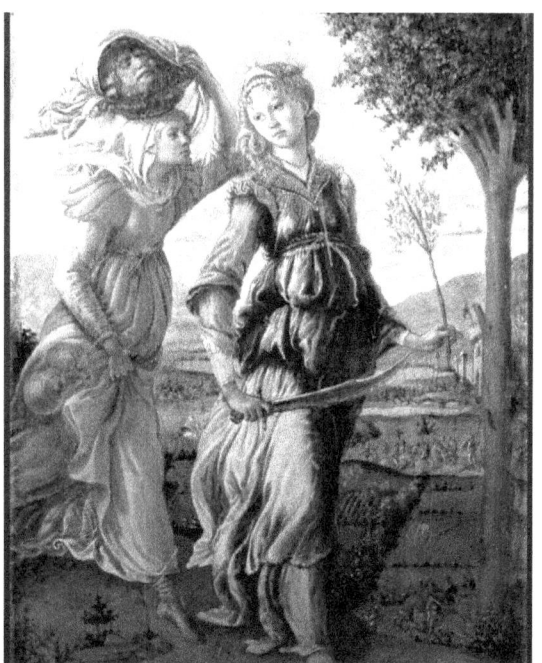

Judith's Return to Bethulia by Sandro Botticelli

He presents his works to Simonetta Vespucci and reveals to her his secrets, the coded messages he skilfully draws and the use of mathematics to give additional strength to his artworks. Simonetta is very clever but she is amazed. She is impressed by this captivating man, so special, so unique in the landscape of the great Florentine families of that time.

CHAPTER 13

In the residence of Vespucci lives Simonetta but also Amerigo Vespucci, her cousin by marriage. Amerigo is a young man of the same age as Simonetta and who, like all Florentines, is also very interested in Greek thinkers, Neoplatonism and who reads Dante. Amerigo often accompanies her cousin Simonetta and often they speak with Sandro Botticelli, the master of Neoplatonism in Florence city. Sandro Botticelli introduces Simonetta and Amerigo to a woman from history whom he considers unique. This woman is called Hypatia of Alexandria. In 400 A.D, she lived in the city of Alexandria, in northern Egypt with its huge library and its legendary lighthouse bordering the Mediterranean. Hypatia is a very beautiful woman who is very clever. She is a mathematician, but also a philosopher and an astronomer. She is a Neoplatonist, that is to say that she comments, like other Greeks of this time of 400 AD, on the texts of Plato written in 400 B.C, 800 years ago.

Neoplatonists are called the new Platos.

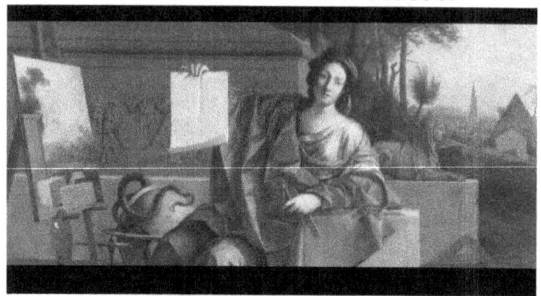

Hypatia of Alexandria

She is also an astronomer and an amazing mathematician who invented an instrument that Sandro Botticelli finds revolutionary, an Astrolabe. This instrument, round in shape like a large coin, is made up of several discs and allows on one side to calculate the exact time and on the other side to calculate the distance between the stars and the Earth.

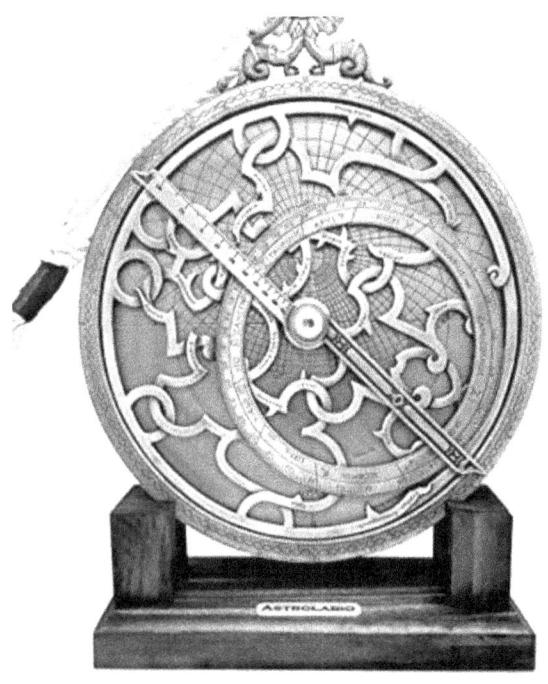

Photo of an Astrolabe created by Hypatia of Alexandria

Simonetta and Amerigo listen with great interest to Sandro Botticelli's stories about this amazing woman, Hypatia of Alexandria. A few days later, at another banquet, Simonetta and Amerigo are talking together and Sandro Botticelli comes, joins them and gives Simonetta a present. He offers her an Astrolabe of Hypatia of Alexandria which he had made by one of his goldsmith friends. Sandro shows Simonetta how to use it. This instrument makes it possible to calculate the latitude, so we know exactly where we are with this instrument.

The process is not so complicated to use, especially since Sandro has good math skills. Simonetta is fascinated by this instrument, this woman, Hypatia of Alexandria, but above all by this man of insatiable knowledge, Sandro Botticelli. Amerigo Vespucci is next to them and attends Sandro's demonstration. In the evening, he begs Simonetta to give him this Astrolabe of Hypatia of Alexandria. Simonetta feels that the approach is sincere and she offers him this instrument, the Astrolabe of Hypatia of Alexandria. I make a parenthesis to tell you briefly the story of this Astrolabe and of Amerigo Vespucci. In the near future, Amerigo Vespucci will travel to Spain and will be one of Christopher Columbus' best friends. He will speak of this Astrolabe to Christopher Columbus who will use Astrolabe to find his bearings at sea on his first voyage to discover the new continent. This instrument makes it possible to calculate the latitude and the positioning at sea as on land thanks to the stars.

After the new continent is discovered, Amerigo Vespucci will make several trips to the new continent, then, he will become the trainer of navigators to cross the Atlantic by teaching them the use of the astrolabe to orient themselves at sea. He will write multiple and varied texts on the " new continent". Then, one day, while cartographers are looking for a name other than "the new world", for this new continent, they will come across the writings of Amerigo Vespucci. As the new continents discovered will be called

"Africa", "Arctica", "Antarctica", amerigo will become "America" to give a name to this new great continent and this name will remain. This Astrolabe used by all sailors of that time will in the future become a Quadrant (¼ of the astrolabe) then in 1700 will be simplified to a Sextant for orientation at sea. End of this parenthesis and the story of this Astrolabe of Hypatia of Alexandria linked to Amerigo Vespucci and Christopher Columbus.

CHAPTER 14

Inexorably, Simonetta draws closer to the seductive Sandro who shows great class by never making her feel uncomfortable. The fire of love and desire begins to grow between these two amazing characters who are constantly closer for their greatest pleasure.

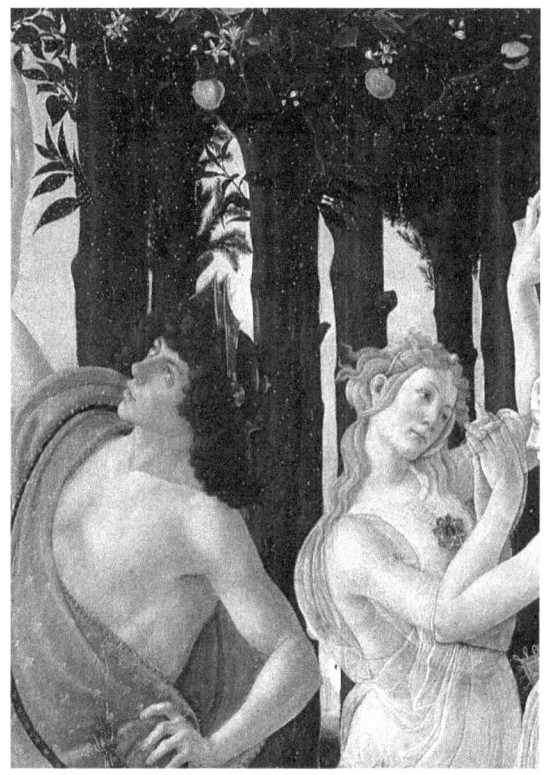

In the painting "Spring", Sandro draws himself next to the one he loves in the many festivities

It is difficult to know when exactly these two characters get out together and what their story is precisely, but this forbidden love is of rare strength and intensity. But, the two lovers must love each other in secret because their life is at stake and especially Sandro's life. Simonetta Vespucci is sheltered and safe due to her rank and her immense beauty, but Sandro, on the other hand, risks death every moment spent with the woman he is madly in love with. But this idea of death, of an execution, does not scare Sandro. Yet, at this time, murders were common in Florence city, with family rivalries still present. Sandro, 29, was not born into a noble family, he is a simple artist whom the powerful italian families can have assassinated with the snap of a finger, without the slightest hesitation. But, Sandro is so in love that he doesn't care about dying as long as he can live this love with the one who makes his heart beat so hard, the one who transports him, who makes his spirit and his soul soar. Simonetta also loves Sandro so desperately that she protects her lover by not letting her feelings show at all the festivities and banquets organized very often in Florence city. She plays her role to perfection and she is transported to another world by finding Sandro in secret.

Obviously the two lovers are developing plans to flee Florence city to live their love in a whole and complete way. But it is difficult for the most beautiful woman in Italy to go unnoticed. This relationship would bring discredit and dishonor to the Vespucci family. They would be hunted all over Europe. It was impossible for them to escape. Ultimate beauty as the worst of burdens. However, they keep this hope of running away together so that they can be free to love each other, without being forced to hide in order to love each other. Only a few relatives and trustworthy people know about the great love story between Sandro and Simonetta. Sandro's artist friends, Perugino and Leonardo are of course in the know, as are other artists and poets from Florence city, notably a writer and poet named Masuccio Salernitano who describes in a book the great love story between Sandro and Simonetta and their impossible destiny that Shakespeare will take up in Romeo and Juliet.

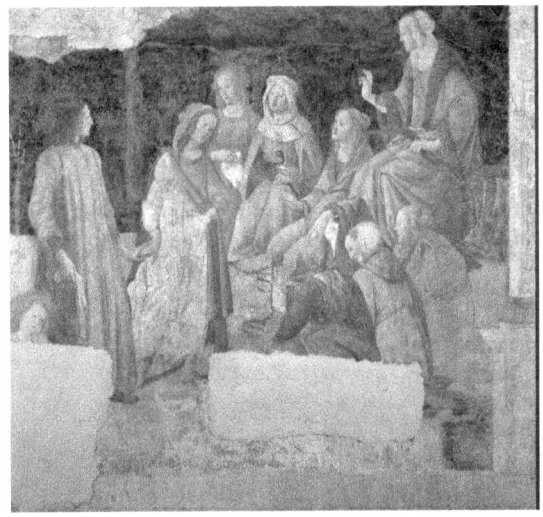

Fresco on a wall of Sandro Botticelli depicting himself with the one he loves.

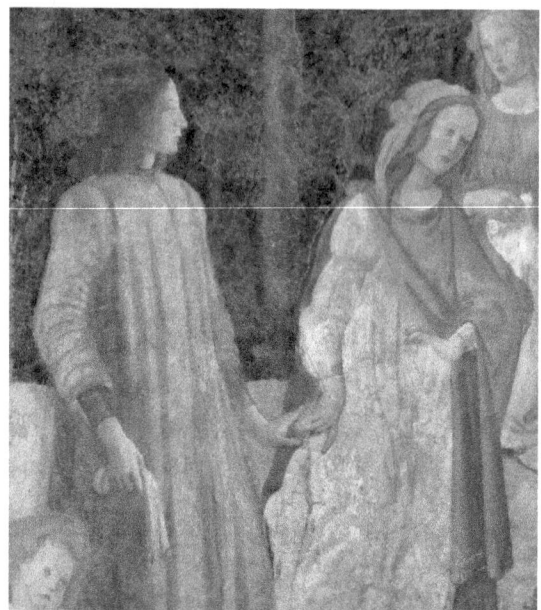

Sandro, red hat, long hair, holds Simonetta's hand.

CHAPTER 15

1475 A.D

A year later, the intensity of their love is still strong but Simonetta faces a new difficulty. Julian de Medici, the little brother of Lorenzo de Medici, 22 years old, is under the undeniable charm of Simonetta and he makes advances to her. Simonetta politely declines Julian's advances but the latter refuses to be turned away and he insists. Julian de Medici is powerful with his brother Lorenzo who governs the city of Florence. Julian wants to own the magnificent Simonetta Vespucci, which he calls "unparalleled". Despite Simonetta's numerous refusals, Julian de Medici insists more and more and persists in becoming annoying and embarrassing by declaring his love for her in a very heavy way. Simonetta is very embarrassed by this suitor who does not want to stop despite the countless refusals on her part. Even Lorenzo de Medici is embarrassed by his brother, but as they had lost their father a few years earlier, Lorenzo indulges him every whim. Thus, even games or horse races become an opportunity for Julian de Medici to try to possess this woman who refuses to do so, but with the dignity of a great lady. Simonetta is going through real hell. A prisoner's life in a golden jail. Her husband Marco goes to see his mistresses, and Julian de Medici, one of the most powerful men in Florence city, harasses her with solicitations, harassing her day after day.

Simonetta finds refuge in the arms of Sandro who respects women and who has something more than all other men in Simonetta's eyes. The desire to escape is strong for them but she is a prisoner of the power of these Italian families. So, while waiting to be free, they live their love with passion and intensity. The meeting of the two forbidden lovers pushing feelings to their height. At night, in Florence city, the two lovers meet again and some people, artists like Perugino and Leonardo who are very close to Sandro, know their friend's secret and are the helpless spectators of this dangerous and forbidden love which would inevitably end badly. Simonetta is harassed by Julian de Medici who is possessively jealous even though he has no relationship with her. He wants to possess her, she would be his thing, his object. But, Simonetta refuses him again and again, which annoys Julian de Medici. Carried by their idyll, the two lovers, Sandro and Simonetta live their love fully and Simonetta poses naked for her lover, Sandro, who paints her in his studio. She loves his talent, his works, his hidden messages, his intellect, his knowledge, his exceptional personality, his assurance, his freedom, his beauty. He also loves her madly. She is a unique, exceptional, extremely charismatic woman, of rare elegance and grace, but she is also of great intelligence. She shines, at the height of her beauty.

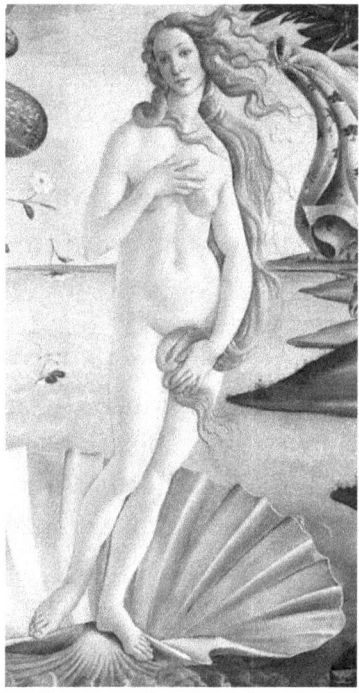

Birth of Venus by Sandro Botticelli

But, after some time, this story of Simonetta posing naked for Sandro Botticelli leaks and the information reaches the ears of Julian de Medici. The texts of the time describe Julian de Medici going into a mad rage on learning that Simonetta Vespucci posed naked in front of Sandro Botticelli. The texts describe him with a sword in his hand, ready to execute Sandro Botticelli for the only official crime of painting Simonetta Vespucci naked. You have to go back to that time with Sandro, 30, at the top, who is endowed with great self-confidence. He was brought up like a Medici since he was a teenager. There is Lorenzo, 26, the new Medici clan leader who is taking over the family business and Julian, 23, a young, brainless man, who thinks he can do anything, the arrogance of believing himself to be the most powerful man of Florence city after his brother Lorenzo. Julian tumbles into Sandro's studio and he tries to intimidate Sandro Botticelli with a sword in his hand forbidding him to paint Simonetta naked. But, Sandro is not at all intimidated by Julian whom he has known since his childhood, quite the contrary, it is Julian who is intimidated by Sandro, the one whom Cosimo de Medici, the grandfather, chose as his spiritual son, the one that Peter de Medici, Lorenzo and Julian's father, also greatly appreciated and had the greatest respect for him, so when Julian arrived with his sword, in the master's workshop, Sandro vigorously chased Julian de Medici from his workshop. Julian, drunk with anger, goes directly to his brother Lorenzo to complain. Julian asks, demands, that Sandro be executed on the spot for not only having painted Simonetta naked but also for having hurt him, the second master of Florence city. But Lorenzo de Medici, who greatly appreciates Sandro, categorically refuses. Lorenzo de Medici refusing to execute Sandro, Julian de Medici, filled with bitterness, seeks another way to avenge himself on Sandro, whose drawings of naked Simonetta come as an offense to this man of unhealthy jealousy. So Julian de Medici decides to hurt Sandro indirectly by attacking his closest artist friends. The one who is in Julian's crosshairs is the young Leonardo Da Vinci, 22 years old.

CHAPTER 16

Early 1476

A most serious accusation is filed with the church court. Accusation true or false, Leonardo Da Vinci is accused of having slept with a man, of having had sexual relations with a man. At that time, in Italy, this act was considered as serious as murder and punished with capital punishment, death at the stake. Leonardo is captured by the church police, the inquisition, and his trial is quickly judged. The man who supposedly was Leonardo's lover was the main witness. Julian de Medici's treacherous trap on Leonardo closes and the sentence falls quickly. On April 9, 1476, Leonardo was found guilty of sodomy and he was condemned to be executed, sentenced to be burned at the stake in a public place. Julian de Medici gets his revenge on Sandro. Obviously, Sandro rushes to see Lorenzo de Medici to ask him to release his painter and artist friend, but Lorenzo de Medici replies that he can no longer do anything to save his artist friend, the ecclesiastical judicial machine has been engaged and no one can prevent the execution of his friend now. Leonardo is condemned to the stake, he will await the execution of the sentence in jail. Much later, in the year 1515, Leonardo pronounced this sentence among the guests of François 1er. Leonardo - "the Medici made me, the Medici destroyed me"

CHAPTER 17

Easter April 26, 1476

Two weeks after Leonardo's death sentence, while he was awaiting his next execution, on April 26, 1476, Easter was celebrated in Florence city. As usual, a large banquet brings together the great Florentine families. The festivities, as usual, praise lavish, gargantuan meals. The demonstration of the power and wealth of the great Italian families.

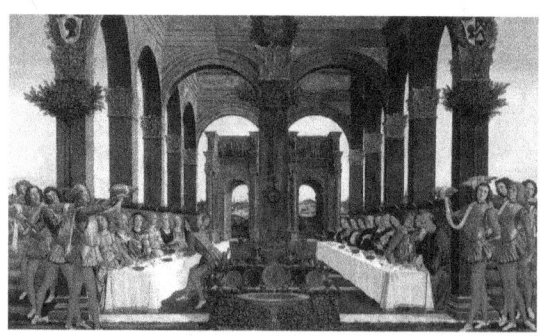

Nastagio degli Onesti by Sandro Botticelli

At this banquet are present Simonetta, the whole Vespucci family, but also the whole Medici family.

Here is the most likely scenario that must have happened: During this banquet, Simonetta disappeared into the nearby forest to find Sandro there. After a last kiss, she begs him to leave which he does. But, as she returns to join the guests, with a smile on her lips, love in her heart, spirit in levitation, happiness in her veins, she comes face to face with Julian de Medici who is approaching her and who grabs her by the arm. Julian de Medici said to her in an aggressive way:
Julian de Medici - *where have you been? I've been looking for you for hours.*
Simonetta, with a quick gesture, removes her arm and says: Simonetta Vespucci - *I wanted to be alone, and anyway, what I do is none of your business. I have no accounts to render to you.* She wants to continue on her way through the forest to the banquet but Julian grabs her arm again and his eyes fill with hatred and anger towards Simonetta. Julian de Medici - *Stop taking me for a fool, I'm sure you were with your lover.*
Simonetta again vigorously frees her arm. She wants to lie as usual but on this specific day, at Easter, in this forest, she decides to tell the truth in front of her stalker.
Simonetta - *it's true Julian, I just saw my lover. I love him and no one else unconditionally. You can imprison*

me or kill me, you will never take away the love I have for him.

Mad with anger at Simonetta's remarks, Julian squeezes a dagger tightly to his belt and, drunk with jealousy, grabs it and stabs her in the chest. She collapses to the ground, the dagger still in the upper part of the bust. During the few seconds she has left to live, she thinks of Sandro and of the unconditional and absolute happiness they experienced in the most perfect of loves. She feels herself leaving but now she is finally free, delivered from this golden prison.

Julian de Medici panics when he sees Simonetta inert, on the ground, in the middle of this forest, dead.

He runs to see his brother, Lorenzo de Medici, seated at the Easter banquet. Julian, in a panic, approaches his brother's ear. He whispers to him, he begs him to come with him. Lorenzo de Medici gets up and, accompanied by a few guards, he follows his brother into this wood just next door. Julian does not dare reveal the tragedy to his brother and he brings him to Simonetta's body.

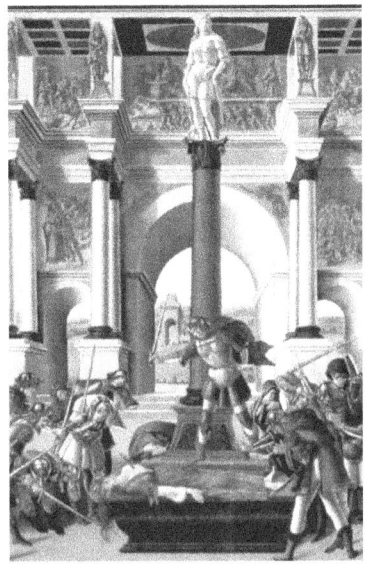

Sandro Botticelli

In the middle of this wood, Lorenzo de Medici and his soldiers see Simonetta, lying on the ground, in her green dress, a dagger in her bust. Terrified, Lorenzo immediately rushes to Simonetta's body with the hope that she is still alive while the soldiers are stunned by this vision. But, quickly, he realizes that she is dead. A nameless drama, a terrible tragedy because Lorenzo de Medici greatly appreciated Simonetta, her beauty, her intelligence, her knowledge, a woman he found amazing in every way. His brother Julian begs his forgiveness, crying. Lorenzo de Medici puts his hands to his face while thinking. His brother Julian has just done something so terrible, so horrible, that his act would put the name of the Medici to shame. All that his grandfather Cosimo de Medici, his father, Peter de Medici and all his efforts also have been ruined by this monstrous, odious and shameful act of his brother. Lorenzo loves his brother very much but he must also and above all save the name of the Medici dynasty from shame and dishonor.

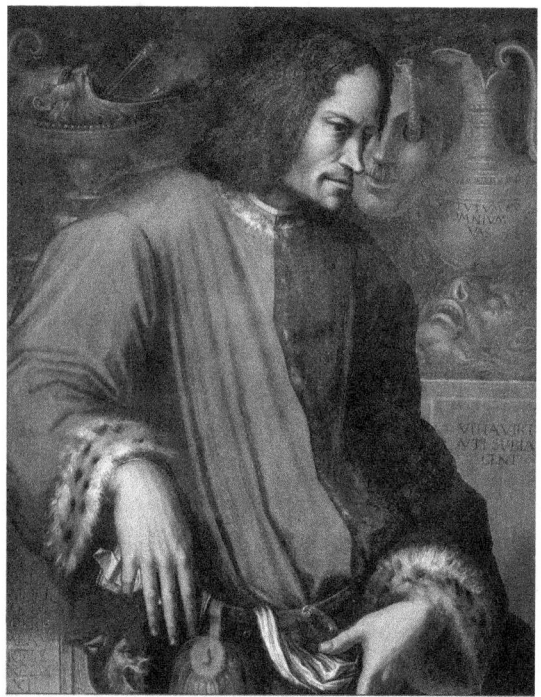

Lorenzo de Medici

There is a lot of excitement at this time, Lorenzo kneeling near the body of Simonetta, Julian crying, gesticulating a lot and the few soldiers who are spectators of this tragic scene. Everyone thinks of the disgrace of the Medici family with this horrible murder.

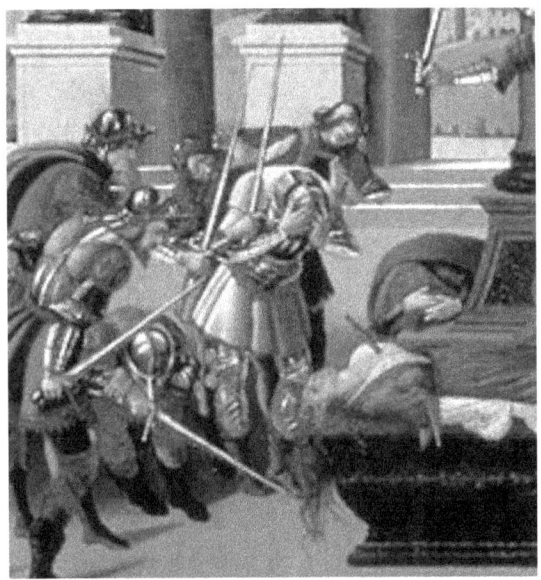

**Painting by Sandro Botticelli
The Weeping Soldiers**

After a few minutes of reflection, Lorenzo gets up and orders two of his soldiers to bring back Marco Vespucci, Simonetta's husband. Julian throws himself at his feet, begging to find a solution and not to abandon him. A few minutes later, Marco Vespucci comes with the two soldiers. Lorenzo shows him the dead body of Simonetta and immediately negotiates with him a solution to this drama, to this problem. Simonetta is dead but Lorenzo must bring the Medici family out of dishonor and shame. The Vespuccis are less wealthy and less powerful than the Medicis and they have been allied families for a long time, several generations. Lorenzo offers a lot of money and power in compensation for the tragedy and asks a big favor from the Vespucci family. A plan is drawn up by Lorenzo de Medici to save the honor and the name of the Medici. Simonetta's body is hidden until evening, then, her dead body is discreetly brought by Lorenzo de' Medici's soldiers to the Vespucci residence with the collaboration and assistance of Marco Vespucci (who will remarry a few months later) and, officially, Simonetta Vespucci dies on the night of April 26, 1476 from overwhelming tuberculosis.

The next day, April 27, 1476, all of Florence spoke only of this tragedy. Simonetta Vespucci, the most beautiful woman in Italy, the pearl, the jewel, the diamond of Florence died suddenly, struck down by tuberculosis during the night. I dare not imagine Sandro Botticelli's reaction when he learned of the death of Simonetta, his love, the woman of his life. I think his first reaction must have been to try to kill himself to reach her if we refer to Shakespeare's novel. Attempts missed or prevented by his artist friends like Perugino, difficult to say but he had to be destroyed.

CHAPTER 18

Two days after the death of the marvelous and sublime Simonetta Vespucci, on April 29, 1476, her funeral took place. The texts mention the grief of the whole city of Florence. All the shops in Florence are closed that day in tribute to this amazing woman who will have marked the history and the city of Florence for eternity. A memorable silence invades the streets of the city. The funeral procession crosses the whole town, then heads towards the Ognissanti church. The texts mention that Sandro is not present in the procession. He is not there. Devastated by grief or in the middle of a suicide attempt, hard to say. In the Ognissanti church, Lorenzo de Medici, who is also a poet, takes the floor to pay a last and vibrant tribute to Simonetta Vespucci and in a magnificent and memorable speech that has spanned the centuries.

Lorenzo de Medici - *"A woman died in our city. Inspiring the universal compassion of all the Florentine people. No wonder. Because, more than any other, she was adorned with authentic beauty and human nobility. Among her many qualities, she had in her way of being such gentleness and such charm that all those who had the privilege of sharing a certain intimacy with her could believe themselves truly loved by her. The other women of her rank not only felt no envy with regard to the excellence of her virtue but they exalted and praised her beauty, her grace, to such an extent that it seemed incredible that so many men could love her without being jealous and that so many women praise her without being envious. And although her life had won her the highest degree of general esteem for her eminent qualities, the compassion caused by death which seized her in the prime of life and the beauty which emanated from her in death, superior perhaps to that of any living creature, will leave a feeling of ardent sadness."*

CHAPTER 19

A few days later, Sandro Botticelli reappears and goes to see Lorenzo de Medici. Here's what they probably said to each other:

Sandro - *Lorenzo, I was Simonetta's lover and I know it was your brother, Julian, who killed her. I wanted to tell you before I divulge the information to everyone.*

Lorenzo de Medici - *Awaits Sandro! Don't do this, I beg you! In the name of my grandfather Cosimo to whom you owe everything, in the name of my father Peter de Medici who loved you like his son, don't do that. Do not bring shame and dishonor on the Medici family! Please Sandro.*

Sandro hesitates because it is true that he owed everything to Cosimo de Medici who was like his spiritual father and he also had a lot of sympathy with Peter de Medici and also with Lorenzo. Sandro - *in the name of Simonetta, I cannot be silent. You must understand Lorenzo, your brother must pay, even if the name of the Medici must be sullied. After all, it's your brother's work.*

Lorenzo adds - *listen to me Sandro, we can find an arrangement.*

Sandro - *I have to tell the truth, I'm sorry.*

Lorenzo de Medici - *listen to me Sandro, you have your artist friend Leonardo da Vinci in jail awaiting execution. I'm offering you a deal, your silence in exchange for his life.*

Sandro hesitates for a moment when he can save the life of his friend Leonardo Da Vinci. He knew that Julian had had him arrested and that he would soon be executed. Sandro knew that Julian had done that to reach him because Julian hadn't supported knowing that Sandro was painting the beautiful naked Simonetta on paintings. Sandro knows that Leonardo is going to be executed for nothing, just because of Julian's jealousy towards him. So, Sandro begins to hesitate in front of Lorenzo's words proposing to repair a deep injustice.

Lorenzo de Medici adds - *I release him in exchange for your patience. His life against your patience to tell the truth. Anyway no one will believe you because I made a deal with the Vespuccis, officially Simonetta died of tuberculosis. Accept this agreement my friend.*

Sandro Botticelli thinks deeply and he adds - "*so my dearest wish is that when I die I want to reside at Simonetta's feet for eternity.*" (This sentence was really proclaimed by Sandro Botticelli).

Lorenzo de Medici - *but this thing is not possible! This is where the Vespucci rest and you are not one of our noble families.*

Sandro - *what do I care! I want to rest with the one I love more than anything for eternity. Take it or leave it.*

Lorenzo de Medici thinks for a few seconds then accepts Sandro's conditions, namely the release of Leonardo Da Vinci and the fact of residing at the feet of Simonetta even if he could also have just executed Sandro Botticelli to silence him. But Sandro is highly respected by Lorenzo de Medici, also called Lorenzo the Magnificent, for whom the values and honor of the Medici family are more important than anything. Cosimo de Medici, Lorenzo's grandfather, greatly appreciated Sandro Botticelli just like his father Peter de Medici and himself, Lorenzo de Medici considers Sandro as a kind of artistic and cultural genius, going beyond the limits of the intellect. So, even if it would have been easier for him to execute Sandro discreetly, he did nothing about it. On the contrary, he accepted from Sandro not only his adventure with Simonetta but also had his friend Leonardo released and honored his commitments to Sandro by continuing to protect him.

CHAPTER 20

Nastagio degli innocenti

Sandro will paint the death of his beloved with a painting in 4 sections entitled "Nastagio degli innocenti". Obviously, with Sandro, everything is always "allegories", hidden messages, even in the titles so you have to refer to this novel in which "Nastagio" appears which tells the story of a very beautiful woman who refuses a noble who desires her very much and, finally she dies, stabbed by a nobleman on horseback. Sandro thus tells the story of the love of his life, Simonetta Vespucci, stabbed by this knight, Julian de Medici, for having refused his advances. Sandro loves allegories, it is necessary to replace the tables in a different order and to add at the end a fifth painting "the tragedy of Lucretius".

It gives this

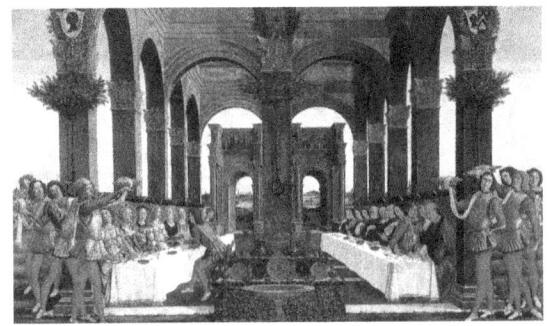

Nastagio degli innocenti part 4
Simonetta on the left, at the Easter banquet,
bothered by Julian de Medici

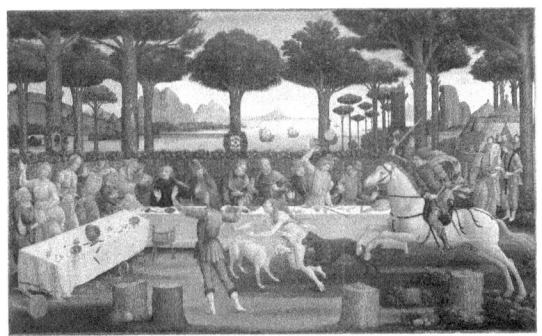

Nastagio degli innocenti part 3
Note that the Medici emblem appears on
the tree. Julian on his horse, sword in hand
chasing the innocent Simonetta

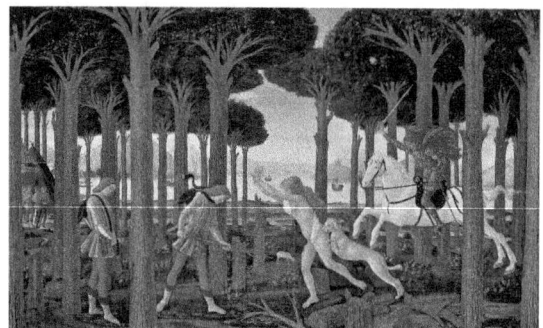

Nastagio degli innocenti part 2

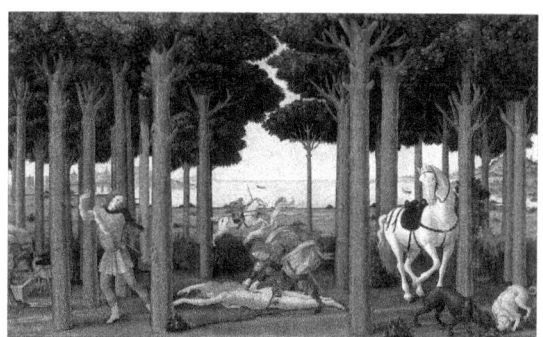

Nastagio degli innocenti part 1
Julian de Medici killing Simonetta

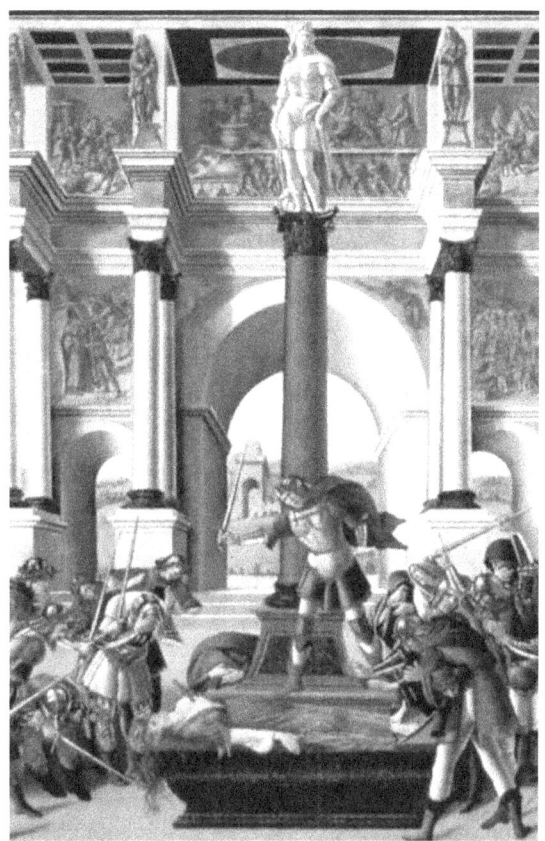

Final painting: "The tragedy of Lucretius".
Simonetta dead, a dagger in the upper part of the body, we can see the distress of the soldiers.

These paintings are painted later, for now Sandro honors his commitments and seeks to free Leonardo.

CHAPTER 21

Saved just in time

Shortly after this interview between Sandro and Lorenzo, just before the execution of the sentence at the stake, Leonardo's trial takes a new turn because the main witness mysteriously disappears. But the church still wants to execute Leonardo. But, under pressure from Lorenzo de Medici, the execution was canceled and then, in June 1476, a month and a half after Simonetta's death, Leonardo was released from jail. I imagine that when he was released, Leonardo must have been welcomed by Perugino and Sandro. It is said little but Leonardo really came very close to execution. He was 24 years old, he was not yet the genius we know today.

CHAPTER 22

1476-1478

It is difficult for me to say what happened during these 2 years. The texts mention that Sandro Botticelli stopped painting for 2 years. Perhaps he was preparing his revenge because here is what happened exactly 2 years after the death of Simonetta Vespucci, on April 26, 1478.

That day, Julian de Medici and his brother Lorenzo de Medici are in the cathedral Santa Maria del Flore to celebrate Easter. A rival family, the Pazzi family, wants to take control of Florence city. They have the support of Pope Sixtus IV to eliminate the Medici. An attack is organized to kill the two brothers, Lorenzo and Julian together. Outwitting the security system and the Medici guards, the Pazzi infiltrate the church where the two brothers are alone. Taking advantage of surprise, they arise on them at lightning speed. Julian is stabbed with 19 stab wounds and quickly dies. Lorenzo is hurt in the throat but he miraculously manages to flee and hide from his murderers. Coincidence or not, Sandro gets his revenge with the brutal murder of Julian de Medici with several stab wounds exactly two years to the day after the assassination of Simonetta. Lorenzo de Medici, a miraculous survivor of this attack, will respond in a bloody and brutal manner. His revenge against the Pazzi family will be terrible. 30 members of the Pazzi family and its allies are executed or hanged in public by Lorenzo de Medici, the other members of the Pazzi family are banished and their property sequestered. Lorenzo de Medici mandates the Vespucci family, his ally, to make an inventory of the property of the Pazzi family and seize it.

CHAPTER 23

1478 A.D

After this incident, life resumes in Florence city. Sandro goes back to painting to immortalize the woman of his life. He paints portraits of Simonetta. His orders are pushed back and Simonetta's paintings follow one another. Sandro wants Simonetta's image to be eternal through his paintings.

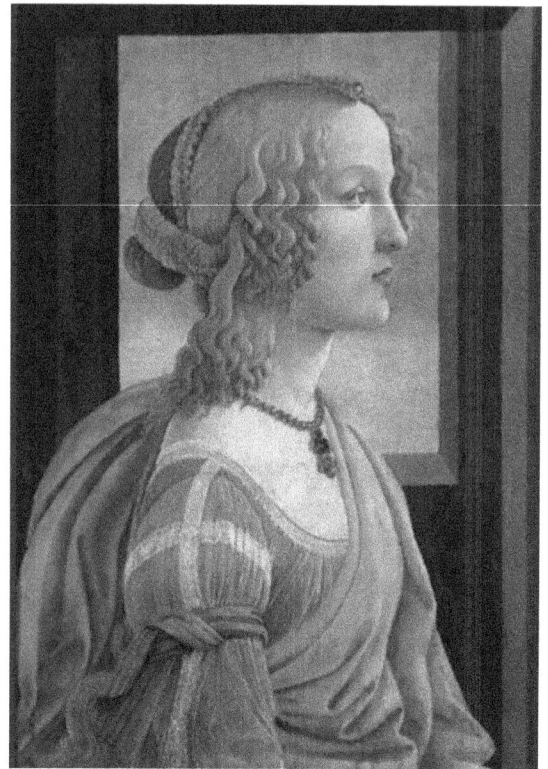

Simonetta Vespucci by Sandro Botticelli

At the same time, Sandro began to learn Greek in order to better understand the texts of Greek mathematicians and philosophers. He also took as a disciple and raised the young Filippino Lippi, the son of his master in painting, Fra Filippo Lippi.

CHAPTER 24

1480 A.D

This year marks a major, revolutionary turning point in painting. At that time, it was forbidden to paint non-religious artworks. All artists who paint non-religious artworks are publicly burned at the stake. The inquisition is still very present, especially in Italy and therefore in Florence city. Sandro will derogate from this fundamental rule and voluntarily infringe this prohibition by presenting a new painting inspired by Greek mythology entitled: "the birth of Venus". In this painting, a portrait of Venus, completely naked, in the guise of her love who disappeared for 4 years, Simonetta Vespucci.

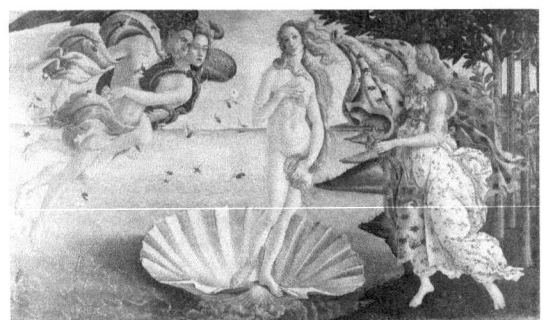

Birth of Venus, by Sandro Botticelli

The painting is a huge success thanks to the amazingly artistic talent of Sandro Botticelli.

The church should have arrested and executed Sandro Botticelli for painting this non-religious artwork, and also a fully nude woman in a painting but Sandro is neither arrested nor executed because he is protected by Lorenzo de Medici and he is so talented that the church accepts the skids of this artist which it needs to decorate the monumental frescoes of the cathedrals. When we talk about the "Renaissance", it begins exactly in 1480 with this painting on Venus by Sandro Botticelli inspired by the neoplatonism initiated by Cosimo de Medici. For the first time in painting history, we move away from Christian religious paintings. A revival in painting that will inspire a whole new generation of artists. But, for the moment, all the artists are not yet following Sandro who is protected by Lorenzo de Medici. Perugino and Leonardo, who narrowly escaped the stake, do not deviate from the obligations of the church to paint religious artworks. But, Sandro persists and paints new non-religious artworks. Thus, he painted just after: "Pallas Athena and the Centaur", always with Simonetta Vespucci as Pallas Athena.

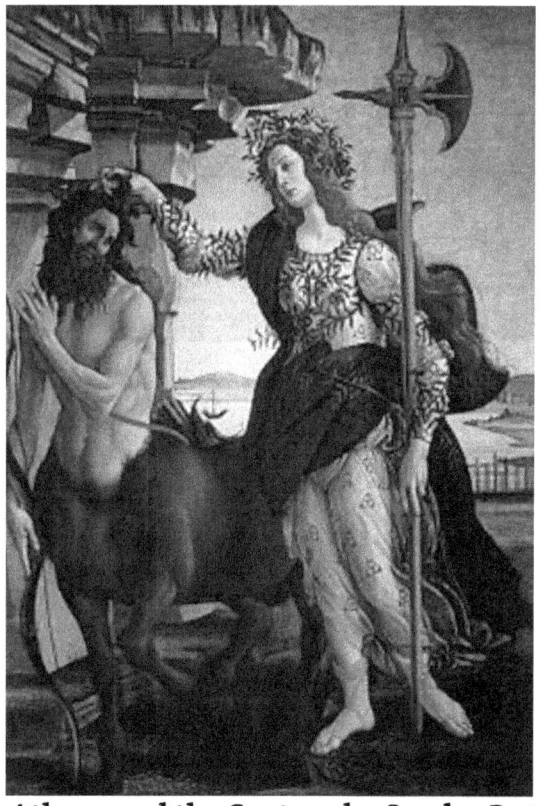

Pallas Athena and the Centaur by Sandro Botticelli

CHAPTER 25

The look

Sandro will go even further and revolutionize the art of this time. In his paintings, one or more characters look at the viewer, the one looking at the painting. Before him, that was not done. In the majority of paintings, religious scenes are painted without anyone looking at the viewer. It is the same for the majority of the portraits, they are done in profile in the vast majority. Sandro revolutionizes this practice by highlighting one or more characters who look at the viewer.

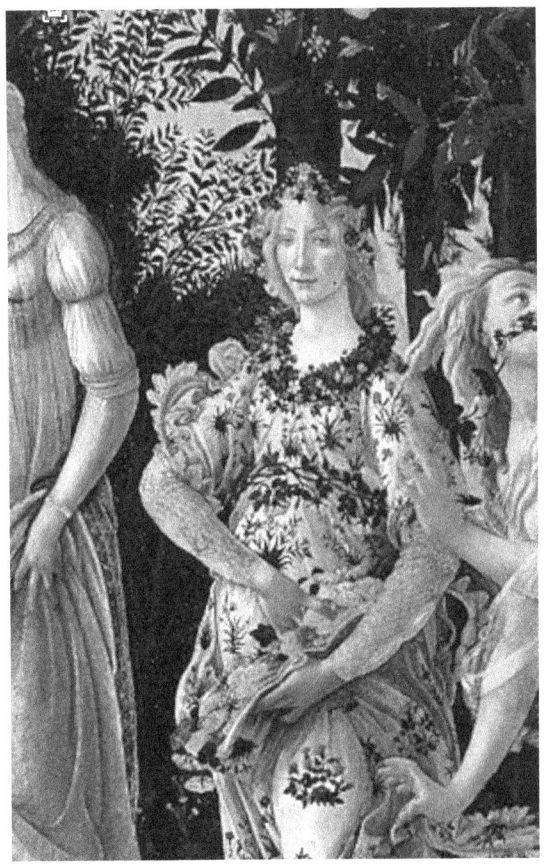

Spring by Sandro Botticelli

Perugino and Leonardo follow Sandro in this practice of major figures who look at the viewer what they did not do before 1480.

Perugino uses this technique very often in his paintings from 1480.

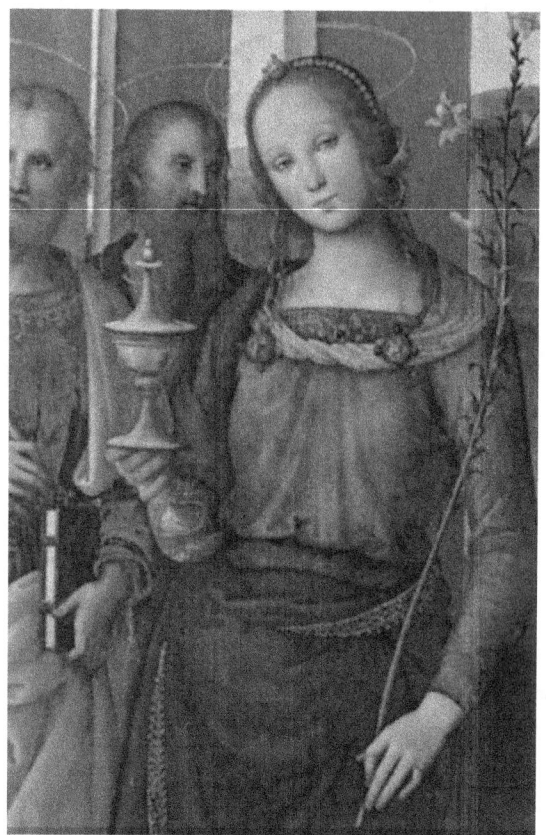

Retable of Fano by Perugino

Leonardo, who narrowly escaped execution at the stake, is more cautious and uses it more rarely.

ROMEO AND JULIET ARE SANDRO BOTTICELLI AND SIMON...

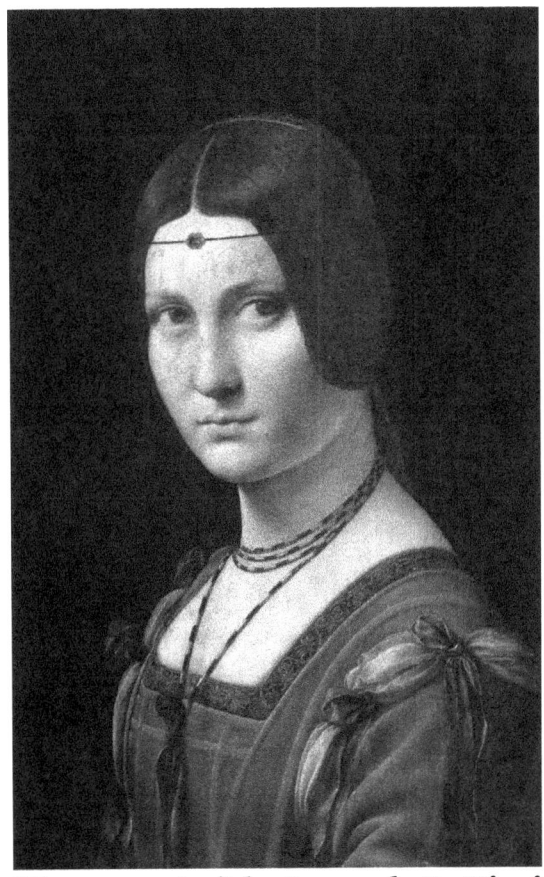

Woman portrait by Leonardo Da Vinci

CHAPTER 26

A book

Always from 1480, Sandro will go even further in the allegories, the hidden messages, by putting in many of his artworks a book. As if to invite you to read, to learn, for knowledge. In his representations of the Virgin Mary, he will begin to put books that Mary, under the face of Simonetta Vespucci, reads. In these religious artworks, this book could be considered as to be the Bible but knowing Sandro Botticelli and his passion for Greek mythologies and Neoplatonism, it is more of a book on Neoplatonist ideas. He invites the viewer of the painting to read too.

Here is a painting of Saint Augustine, a Christian but also Neoplatonist saint who put the Christian religion on a par with Plato's philosophy.

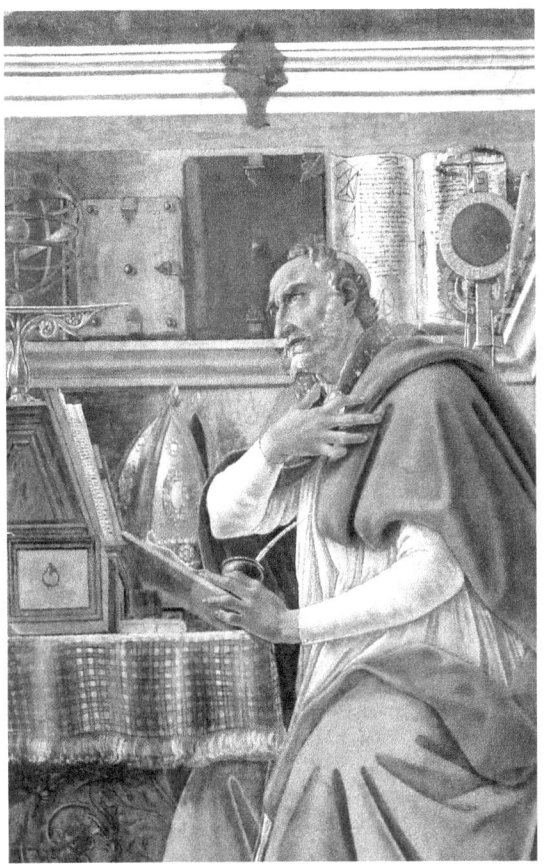

**Saint Augustine by Sandro Botticelli
(Note the open book at top right with
geometric figures drawn on it)**

Perugino and Leonardo also rush into these allegories of the book as the instrument of knowledge and do like Sandro by putting books in many artworks. Perugino does this very often, Leonardo is more discreet in allegories, he will never forget death row.

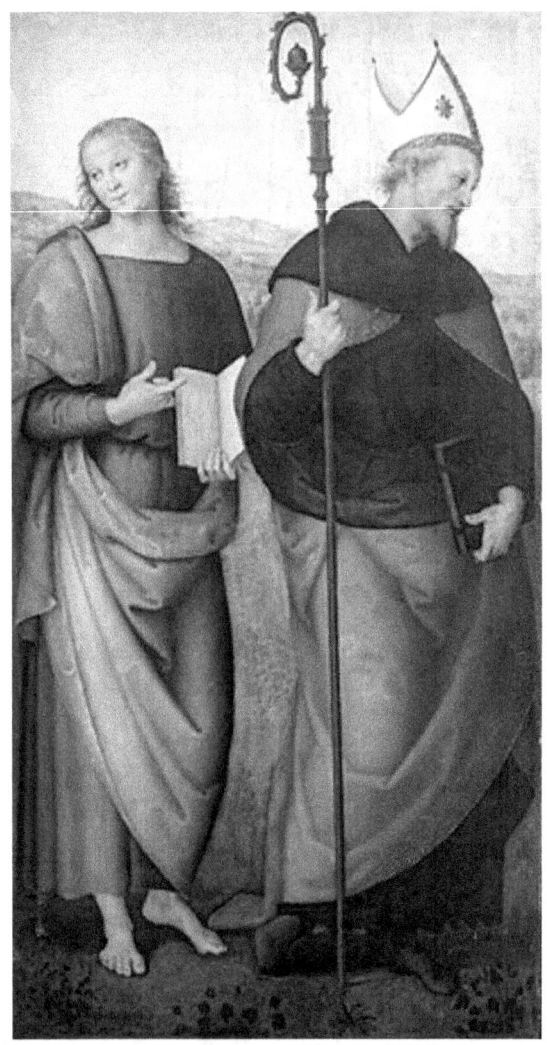

Saint Augustine the Neoplatonist by Perugino

But it is especially with the Virgin Mary, in the guise of his love, Simonetta Vespucci that Sandro Botticelli will most represent a woman with a book, like an invitation to knowledge.

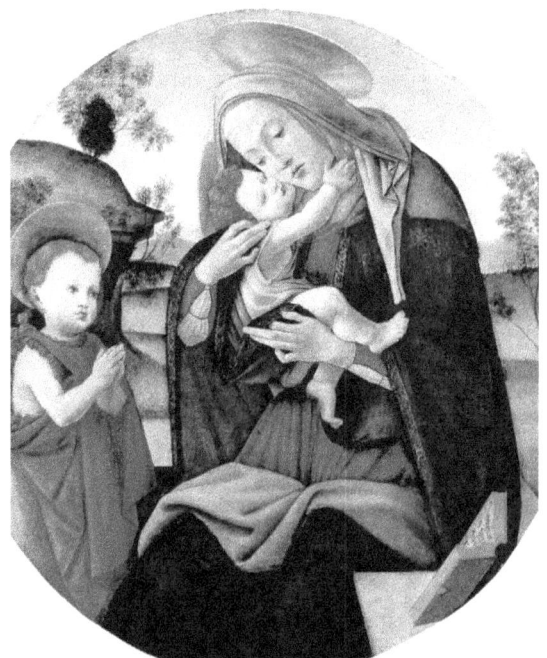

Sandro Botticelli

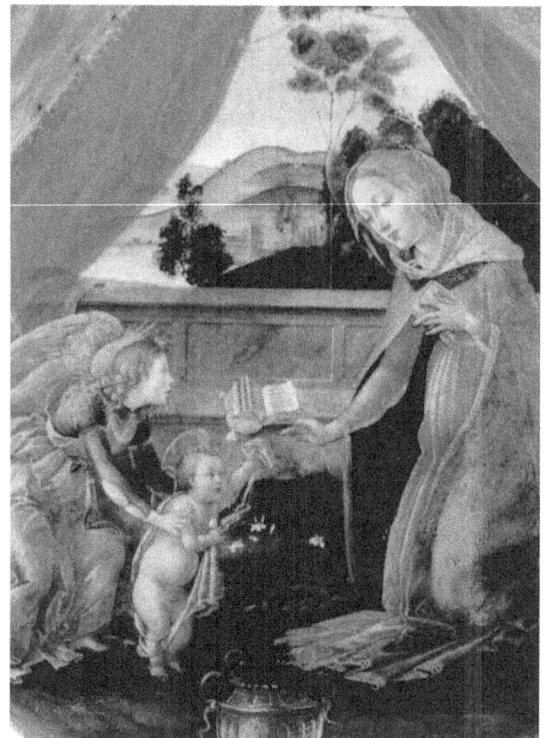

Sandro Botticelli

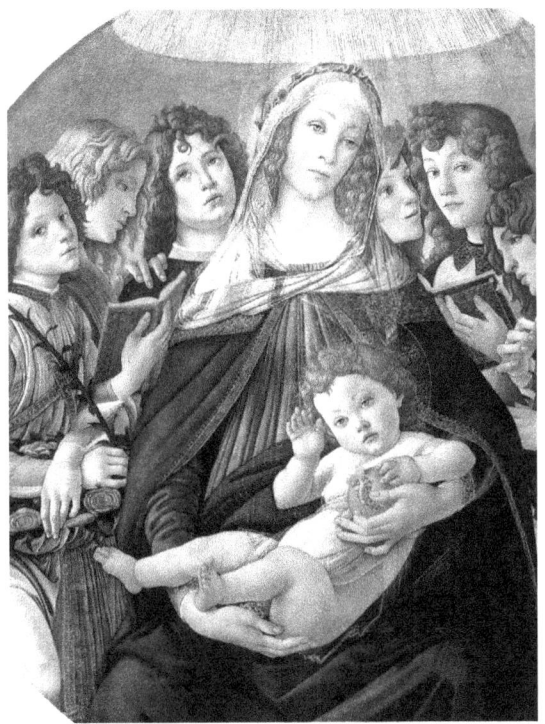

Sandro Botticelli

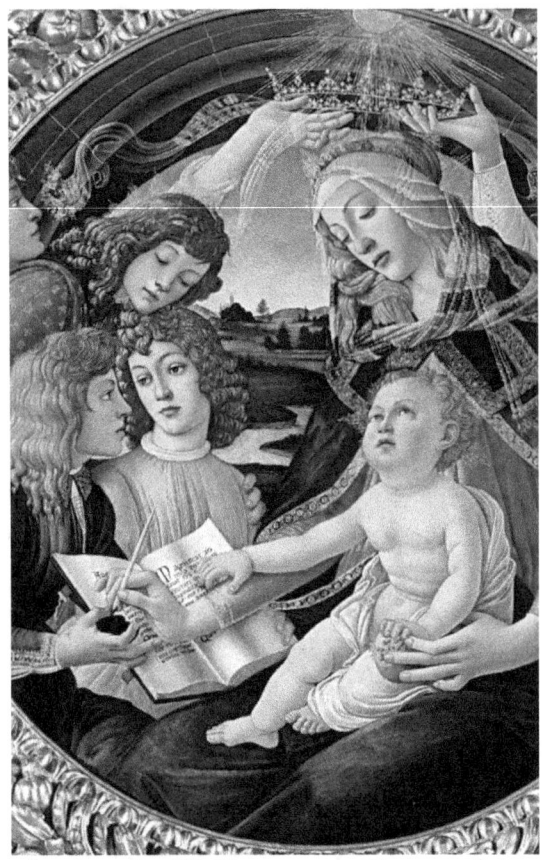

Sandro Botticelli Simonetta Vespucci, in the guise of Marie, even writes something.

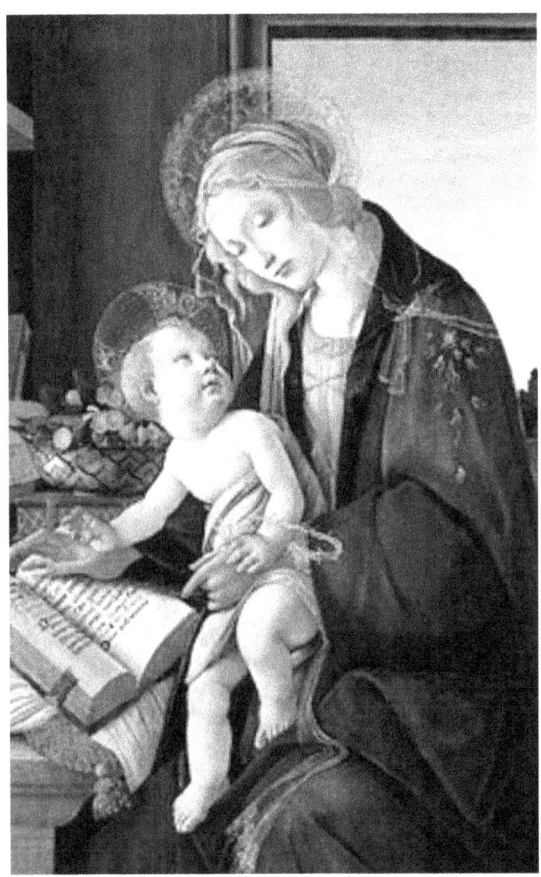

Sandro Botticelli

STEPHANE BAILLON

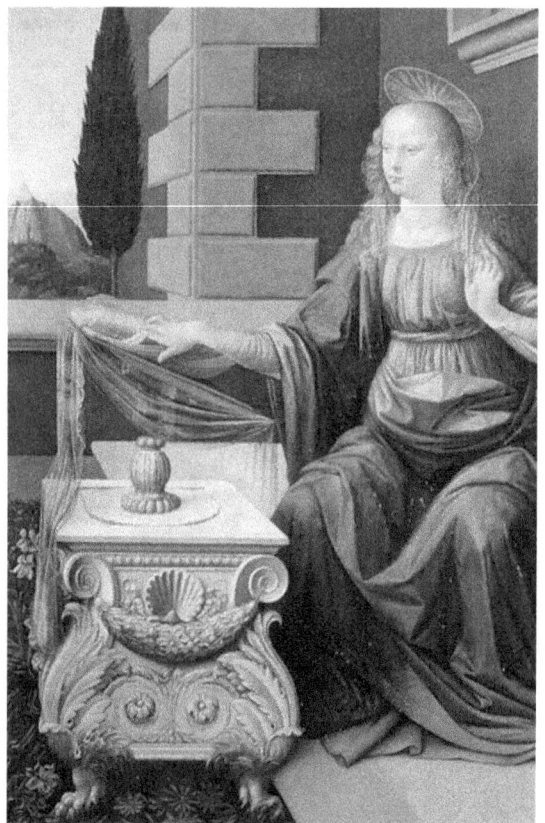

Leonardo Da Vinci

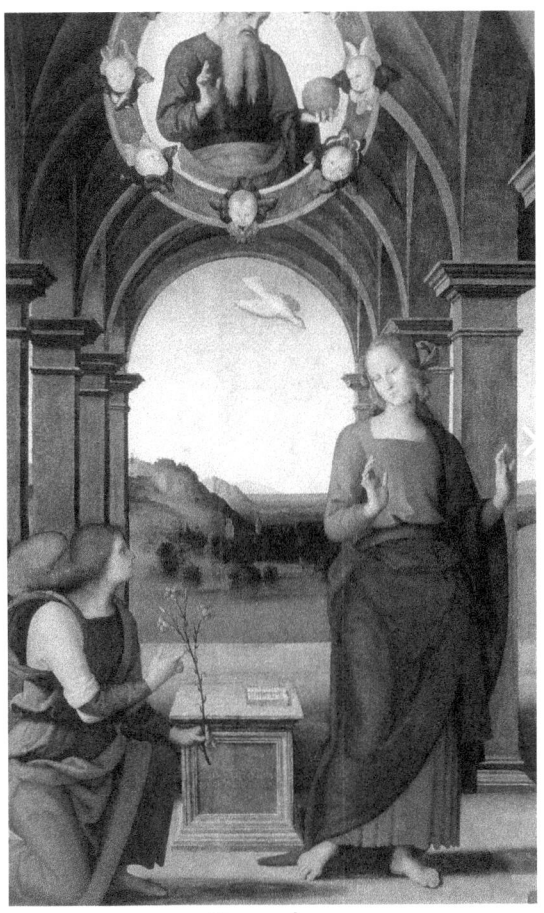

Perugino

STEPHANE BAILLON

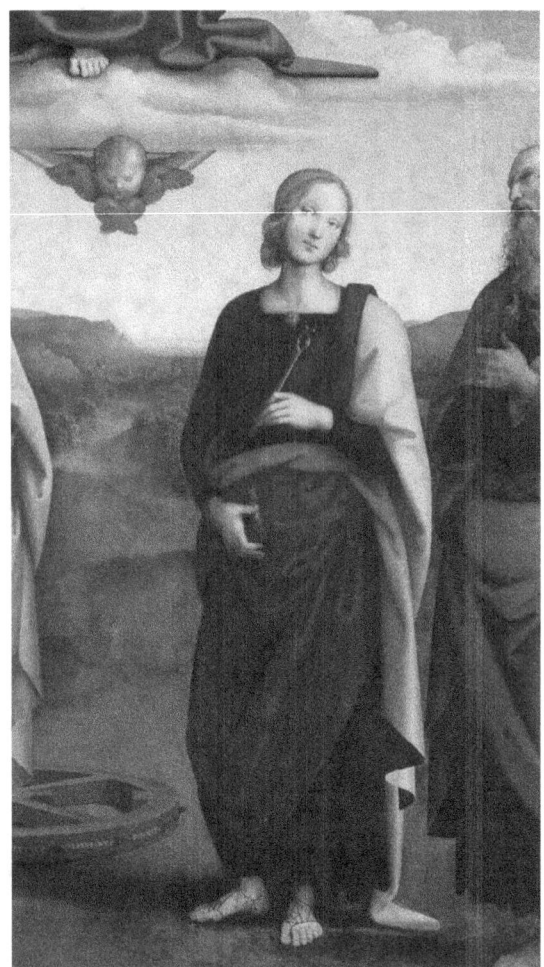

Perugino

ROMEO AND JULIET ARE SANDRO BOTTICELLI AND SIMON...

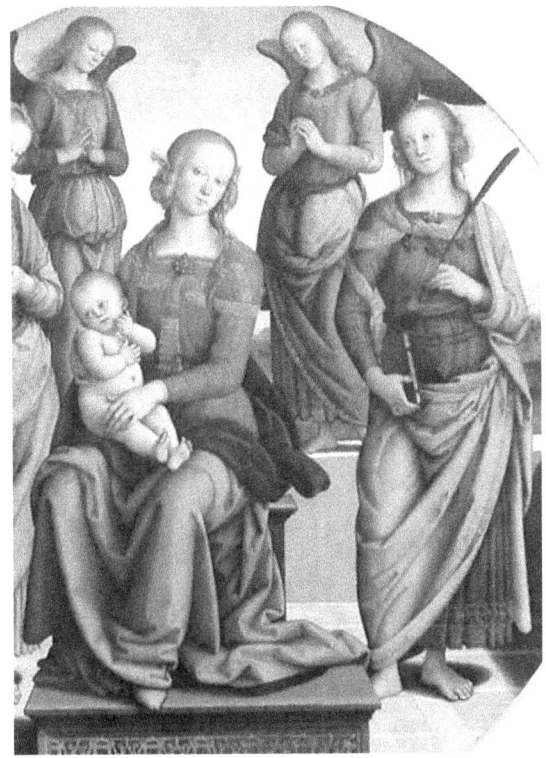

Perugino

STEPHANE BAILLON

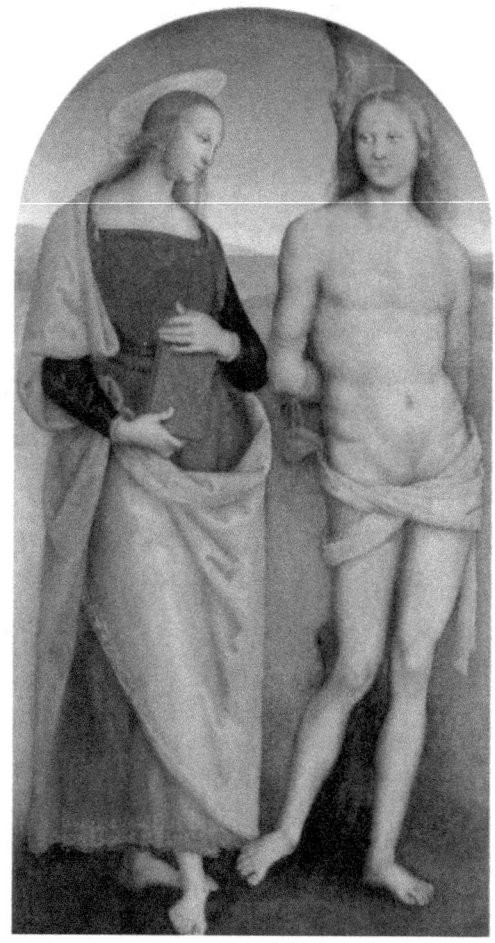

Perugino

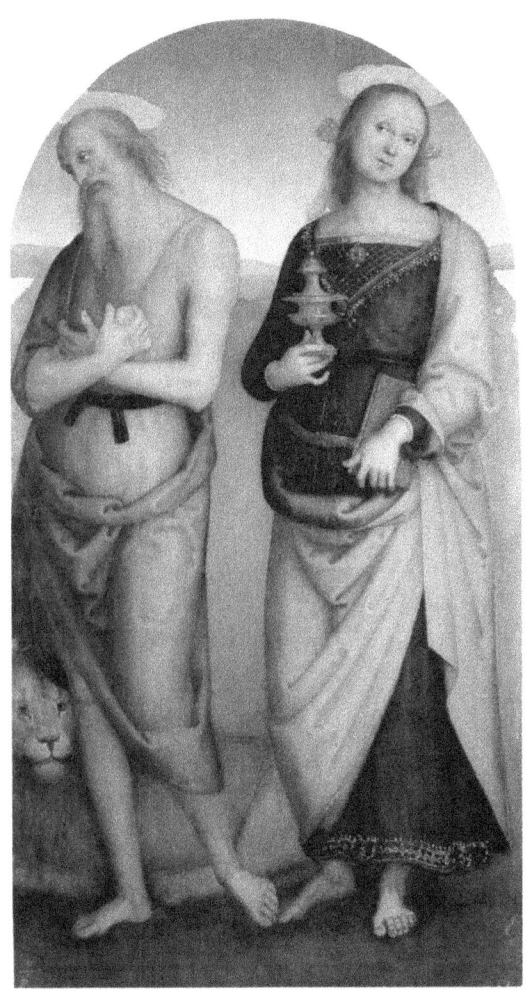

Perugino

CHAPTER 27

1481 A.D

Already three years that Lorenzo de Medici is at odds with the Church and Pope Sixtus who had supported the Pazzi family in his attempt to kill the Medici family. But, Lorenzo the Magnificent decides to renew the dialogue with the pope and as a goodwill in peace agreements, Lorenzo sends the best artists of Florence city to carry out frescoes on a new building next to the basilica San Peter, the chapel Sistine. Sandro Botticelli is the leader of these Florentine artists. He takes with him his pupil, Filippino Lippi but also Perugino and Leonardo who are also on the trip like many other Florentine artists. Sandro Botticelli is the first artist to paint in this Sistine Chapel. This chapel has a strange peculiarity, it is built according to the mathematical rule of the golden ratio used by the Greek Neoplatonists. Sandro produced the first frescoes there, as did Perugino. Leonardo painted the Saint Jerome of the Vatican in this period. But, Sandro does not like the political climate of Rome and he is very impatient to go back to his city, Florence. So, as soon as the frescoes were done, he decided to return back to Florence city and left Rome without even waiting to be paid.

CHAPTER 28

From 1481 to 1492

For more than 10 years, Florentine artists, led by the amazing Sandro Botticelli, painted religious artworks with hidden Neoplatonist messages. Their technique is refined and extraordinary artworks are created during this period that history will call the "Renaissance". Sandro's artworks reach an artistic paroxysm with the representations of Simonetta Vespucci as the Virgin Mary, a book in her hand, a crown above her head, integrated mathematics, games of gaze, fingers pointing at other clues. Sandro raises Simonetta Vespucci as muse, patroness, figurehead of Neoplatonism. This fact is so marked in him that many other Italian artists will rush into this "Simonetta Vespucci" breach. Indeed, these paintings, these portraits of Simonetta Vespucci are not censored by the church and the ecclesiastical power, so all the artists who want to convey secret messages call their paintings Simonetta Vespucci.

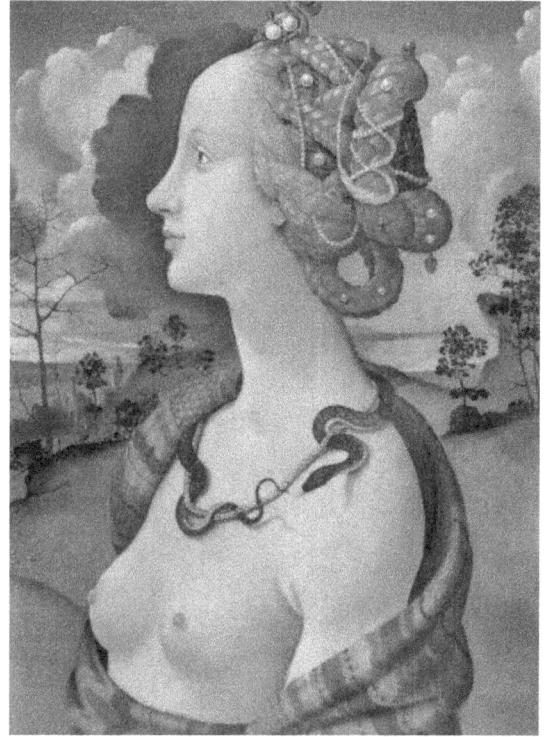

Simonetta Vespucci by Piero di Cosimo

As the Pope had allied himself with the Pazzi to eliminate Lorenzo de Medici, the severity of the Christian religion no longer applied to Florence city during the reign of Lorenzo de Medici, called "Lorenzo the Magnificent", leaving a free field, a boulevard, to the artistic creativity of all these artists, poets and writers. With the neoplatonism of Cosimo de Medici in Florence, with the presence for 30 years of Italian humanists, philosophers and mathematicians and the Christian religion pushed aside, ideas and thoughts are moving away from religion for the first time in a very long time. We are in full expansion of this artistic, literary and free-thinking movement that history will call the "Renaissance". Sandro Botticelli is the centerpiece of the Renaissance, the central character with Lorenzo de Medici as protector. Extremely talented new artists are appearing. Perugino took the young Raphael as his disciple and Lorenzo de Medici welcomed Michelangelo, the new prodigy of sculpture and painting, into his apartments in Florence city. Both, Michelangelo and Raphael, bathed in the neoplatonism of Florence and of course the inevitable influence of Sandro Botticelli.

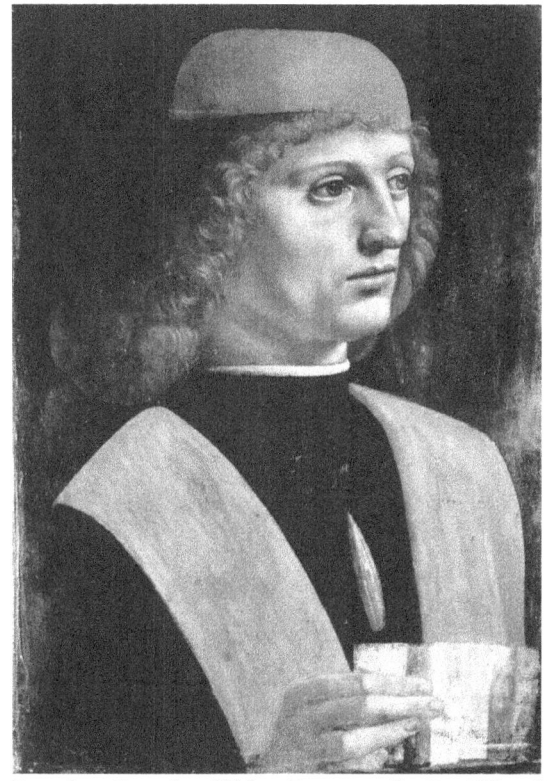

Sandro Botticelli by Leonardo Da Vinci
Officially, according to historians, this painting would represent Franchini Gaffurio, a musician, but it is obvious that it is Sandro Botticelli. The red hat, the long curly hair, the tight black collar, the painter's black apron with that Medici red, holding a text in his hand, that's Sandro Botticelli.

CHAPTER 28

1492 A.D

Lorenzo de Medici is ill and dies. After almost 23 years of freedom, bathed in artistic and literary creativity with neoplatonism, the city of Florence loses its best protector. Lorenzo the Magnificent will have been the worthy successor of his grandfather Cosimo de Medici and his father Peter de Medici.

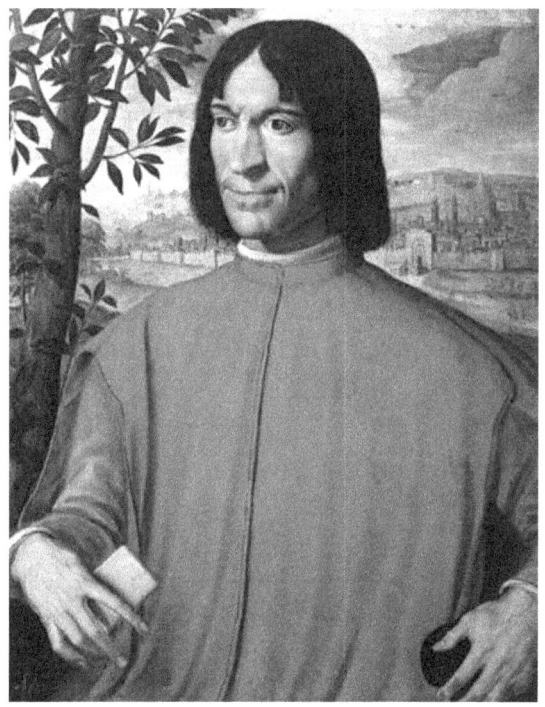

Lorenzo de Medici

The church and the pope take control of the city and put at its head an extremist orator monk called Savonarola. Perugino and Leonardo come to see Sandro Botticelli.

Leonardo - *come with us Sandro, we have to flee Florence, the Church has dreamed for too long of recovering this city considered dissident with the neoplatonist ideas that are spreading there. They will want to return to exclusively religious pictures and ideas, that's obvious. Me, Leonardo, I go to Milan which offers me protection, come with me otherwise you could end up at the stake.*

Sandro - *thank you my friend but I love my city too much and I will find an arrangement with the church which often orders me.* Perugino - *Leonardo is right my friend, you should flee Florence city. Me, Perugino, I go to Mantua where an amazing woman called Isabella d'Este offers me asylum. She is in the process of taking up the torch from Cosimo, Peter and Lorenzo de Medici, she knows the Neoplatonists and she is our ally. She welcomes humanists, poets, artists like us to Mantua. I even have a workshop there.*
Sandro - *thank you my friends but I will not leave Simonetta and Florence city, even if I have to die there.*

From 1494 to 1497, Savonarola endeavored to erase all that the Medici family had done for all these years. He tries to destroy neoplatonist ideas by imposing the Christian religion in its strictest way.

On February 7, 1497, the "pyre of the vanities" took place in the center of Florence city. After an extremist religious speech, Savonarola sends the children to search into all the houses in Florence city and asks them to bring back everything that Savonarola considers sinful to burn on a huge brazier. There is make-up, dresses, musical instruments, but above all books, poems, non-religious writings, mythology paintings and nudes. Sandro Botticelli did everything to avoid this destruction but, to safeguard his most important paintings, in which there are the most hidden messages, he brings some of his paintings which he throws into the fire. A heartbreak for Sandro, who, as he had been warned by Leonardo and Perugino, had not succeeded in opposing the all-powerful Christian church and especially this extremist monk Savonarola. An artistic and literary lost with the destruction of artistic and literary artworks of inestimable value. But, this religious inferno was so extremist that just after the pyre of vanity, Savonarola started having problems with Pope Alexander VI. Finally, shortly after, the extremist monk Savonarola is judged of heresy and is sentenced to be burned at the stake in a public square. With the death of Savonarola, calm returns slowly to Florence city but Sandro had to sacrifice some of his artworks to save the others and this religious state of mind traumatized him. He didn't think religion could go so high in destruction. Now he would hide clues in religious artworks because at least they would not be destroyed by religion. But Sandro is getting old now and paints a lot less. Moreover, he is falsely accused of having agreed with the ideas of Savonarola, when this incredible neoplatonist artist was at the antipodes of the extremist Christian religion. He will paint in response this canvas entitled the calumny of Apelles because like him, Apelles, a Greek painter living under Alexander the great, had been falsely condemned in public before proving his innocence but, Sandro, like Apelles will suffer this injustice the rest of his life.

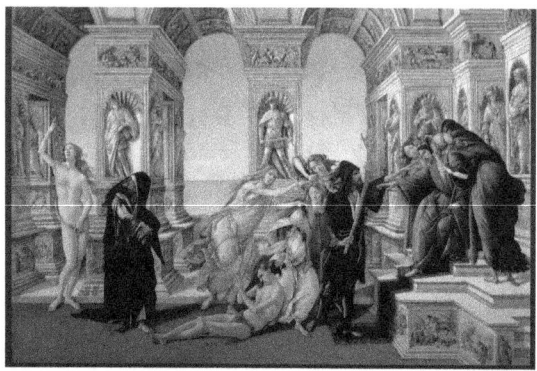

The Calumny of Apelles by Sandro Botticelli

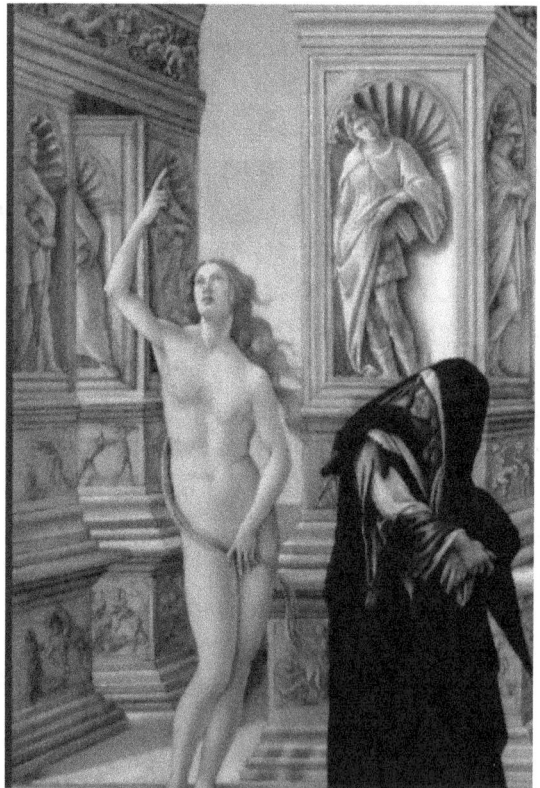

Ecclesiastical power against the nudes

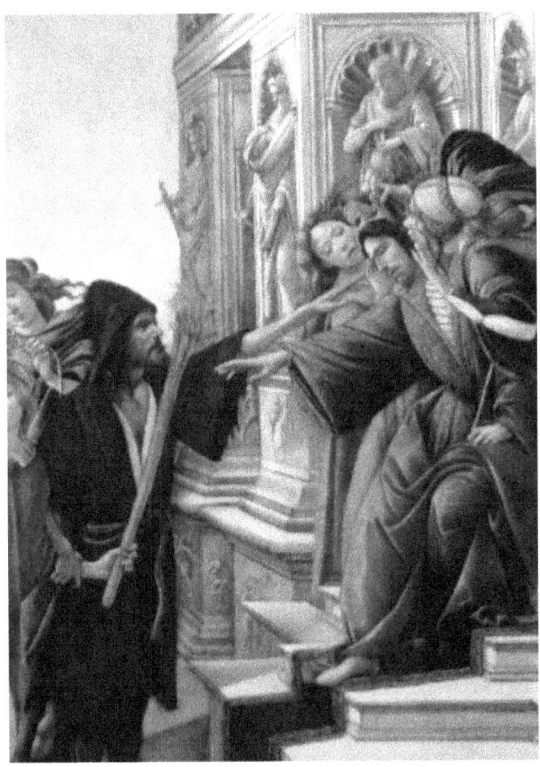

Savonarola on the left and his stake, opposite him Lorenzo de Medici on the right

CHAPTER 29

Isabella d'Este

As Perugino had said, Isabella d'Este became at this time the new protector of artists, poets and writers of the Renaissance. She collects more than 40,000 artistic artworks from the Renaissance. Perugino lives in her castle and has his studio in which Raphael, his young pupil, works. Sandro comes to Mantua and he meets Isabella d'Este. He immediately understands that she is a woman, a collector, an amazing intellectual person. A correspondence is tied between Isabella d'Este and Sandro Botticelli which will last until his death.

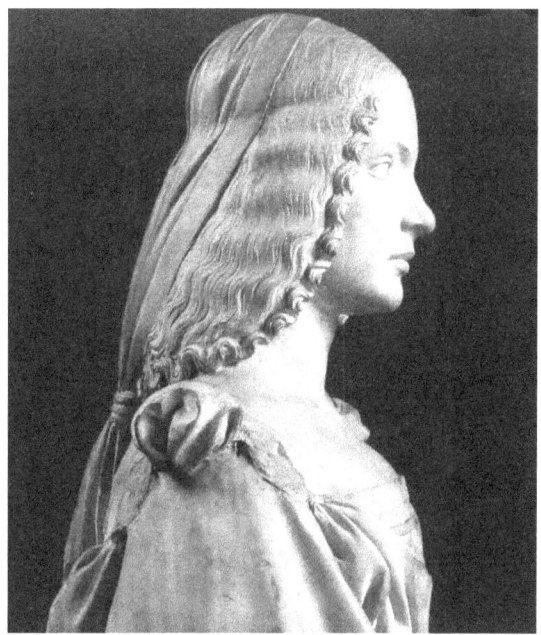

Statue of Isabella d'Este

Leonardo also comes to Mantua and also meets Isabella d'Este. As for Perugino and Sandro, Leonardo greatly appreciates Isabella d'Este who introduces Leonardo to a mathematician named Luca Pacioli. Leonardo, who is already very strong in mathematics, meets a master of mathematics and together they work diligently on mathematical projects. Leonardo comes to see Isabella d'Este and confides to her:

Leonardo - *I have made such discoveries in mathematics that I completely abandon my brushes.* (Sentence really pronounced by Leonardo to Isabella d'Este). After months of research, Leonardo and

Luca Pacioli wrote a mathematics book together entitled: "De divina proportione".

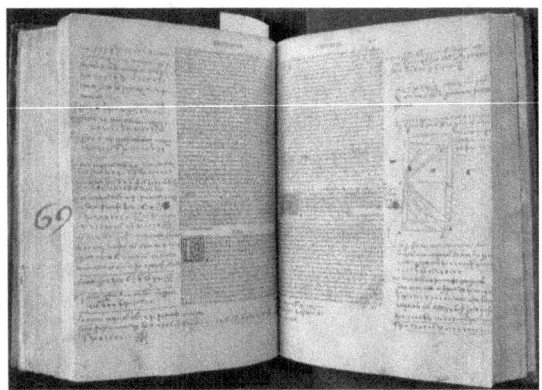

Book De Divina proportione

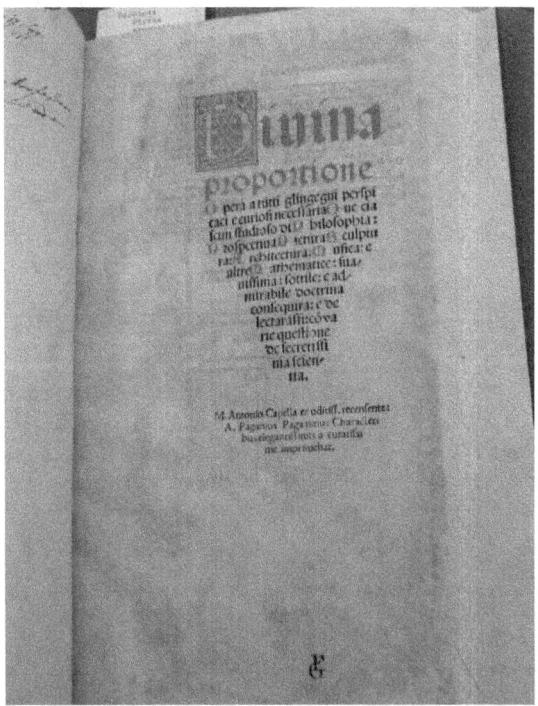

Original presentation of the book by Leonardo and Pacioli. Please note the visual resemblance to the painting of Dante's Hell by Sandro Botticelli and the name above all: De Divina proportione very close to De Divina commedia from Dante.

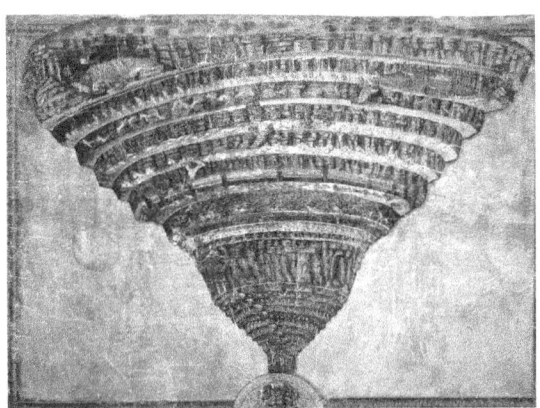

Dante's Inferno by Sandro Botticelli

It must be said that Dante is the first to have used mythologies and is a model for all poets, writers, painters and artists in Florence city, and Dante was also Florentine.

Isabella d'Este is really the character who takes up the torch after Lorenzo de Medici for all the artists and poets of this period. She is a major character of this era in the art world.

STEPHANE BAILLON

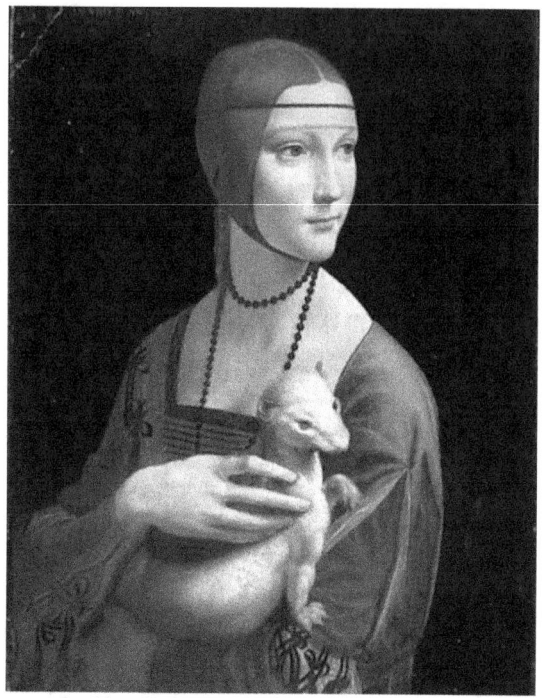

Isabella d'Este by Leonardo Da Vinci

CHAPTER 30

Sandro is old, poor and physically impaired. He doesn't paint much anymore. Traumatized by the destruction of his artworks by the church, he sends all his last paintings directly to Isabella d'Este in the hope that they will not be destroyed by extremist monks like Savonarola.

1503, Sandro is 58 years old, he meets Leonardo in Florence city and they both ask Michelangelo, 28 years old, to try to make a sculpture with a marble block which has just arrived. Michelangelo is a genius whose model is Sandro Botticelli. Michelangelo is captivated by the Greek mythology of Sandro Botticelli. Michelangelo is the artist whose genius and talent is so strong that he will put in his paintings many Greek myths while this is formally prohibited by the Church. But, like Sandro in his time, he is an artist so well known for his talent and so valuable to the pope and the church that his artworks are not destroyed. With the marble block of Sandro and Leonardo, Michelangelo creates an Apollo from Greek mythology.

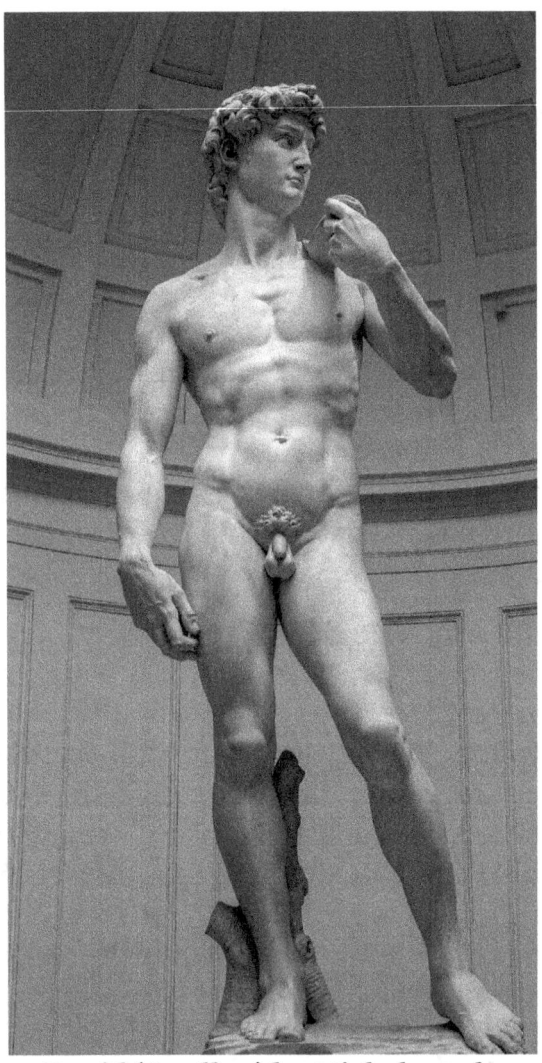

**David (Apollon) by Michelangelo
1503**

Apollo is always depicted naked in mythology. This sculpture is 4.30 meters high, with a snake on its shoulder as in mythology. An artwork, an amazingly beautiful and enigmatic sculpture. Michelangelo achieves a masterpiece of power from the king of the Greek gods. The statue is magnificent, but Michelangelo speaks to Sandro because both are afraid that the statue of Apollo will be destroyed by religion, as happened with Savonarola.

Sandro tells him - *just change Apollo's name to another in the bible.*

Both begin to look at what bible name to give this character. They see David's name and his slingshot.

Sandro says to Michelangelo - *if you flatten the snake's head a little, you can tell it's a slingshot.* Michelangelo - *yes but it's still too obvious, David with the slingshot was a child and there Apollo is a man and of course completely naked which David was not.*

Sandro - *don't worry Michelangelo, it will pass like that I'm sure of it, believe me.* Michelangelo - *yes, but if I want to say that it was Apollo that I represented.*

Sandro - *just write an added sentence.*

Michelangelo - *you are right, I will say "what David did with his sling, me, Michelangelo, I did with my bow"(true sentence said by Michelangelo describing this statue).*

Sandro - *it's very good to say bow instead of your sculpting instrument, the most erudite will easily understand that you meant Apollo and his legendary bow, well played.*

Throughout his career, Michelangelo will go more and more towards the mythology of Sandro through his paintings such as on the ceiling of the Sistine Chapel.

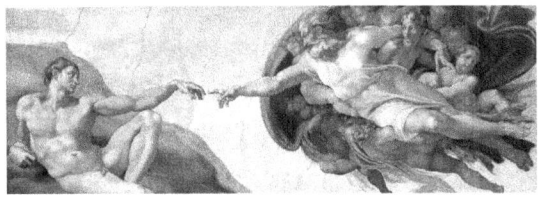

or his sculptures such as this Apollo David made in 1530.

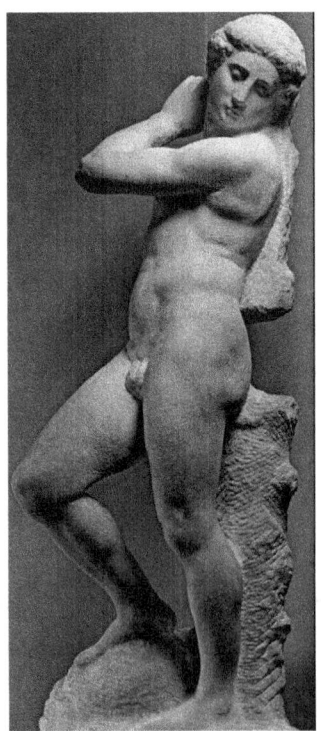

Statue titled "Apollo-David" by Michelangelo 1530.

Other artists will continue, for decades, to honor this genius of Sandro Botticelli by allusions, diverse and varied allegories.

The very talented Raphael, Perugino's pupil, will also pay homage to Sandro Botticelli in his painting entitled "The School of Athens".

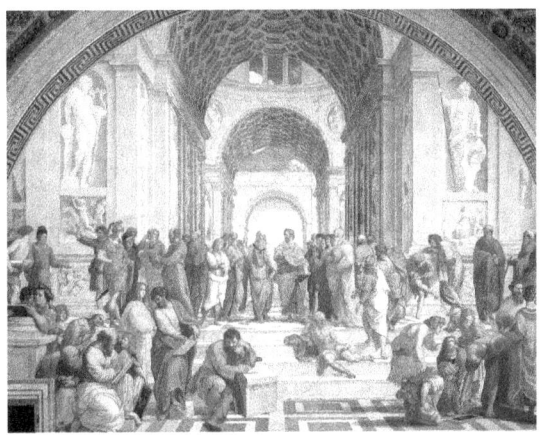

School of Athens by Raphael, 1508-1512

We see 50 philosophers with Plato in the center and one character is looking at the viewer.

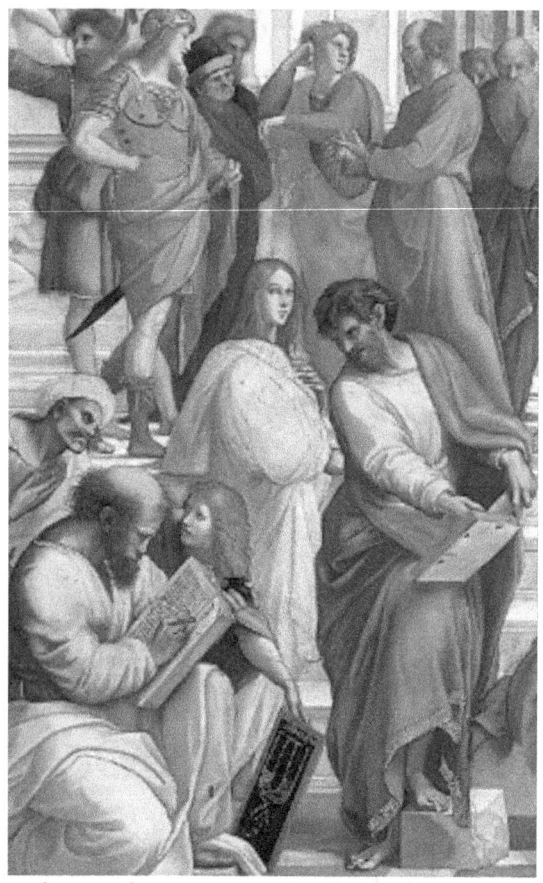

She is the only one to look at the spectators, she is drawn in the image of Simonetta Vespucci and represents the mathematician, astronomer, philosopher and Neoplatonist Hypatia of Alexandria.

CONCLUSION

Sandro Botticelli will have been the central, unavoidable character, the great star of this entire era from 1480 to 1500 in Florence city, Italy. He is at the origin of this artistic revolution in painting that history will call the "Renaissance". Leonardo Da Vinci, Perugino, Raphael, Michelangelo were all deeply inspired by Sandro Botticelli and many more in the future. He will influence the great Flemish painters then French classicism and this craze for mythology at the time of Napoleon in 1800.

Sandro Botticelli died in 1510 and, in accordance with his dearest wish which he had constantly proclaimed throughout his life, his remains were buried at the foot of the tomb of Simonetta Vespucci, in the church of Ognissanti in Florence city.
Romeo, after all, joins Juliet for eternity.

The End

www.ingramcontent.com/pod-product-compliance
Lightning Source LLC
Chambersburg PA
CBHW071414210526
45465CB00001B/383